Observations from readers of Medicine Words

Medicine Words is a book of 10,000 healing incantations, lovingly whispered by master healer Dianne Connelly. Dr. C seamlessly blurs the line between all those mighty kindnesses she has received and those she artfully recycles and augments to transform human suffering into joy — a mouthed recipe for wholeness, delicious for patient, clinician, and reader alike.

> — REBECCA ALBAN HOFFBERGER
> Founder and Director, American Visionary Art Museum

Dianne Connelly's work is like fireworks on a summer night, exploding with the love of life, and, after each treatment, leaving those in her care with a more humane, more compassionate peace.

> — JOHN G. SULLIVAN, PhD
> Powell Professor of Philosophy Emeritus at Elon University,
> author of *Living Large,* and most recently, *The Spiral of the Seasons: Welcoming the Gifts of Later Life*

In *Medicine Words,* Dianne Connelly calls me to be aware, at times painfully, of the impact of my speaking on all who hear the sound of my voice. Speaking well demands courage and mindfulness.

> — ROBERT DUGGAN, MA, MAc (UK)
> President, Tai Sophia Institute,
> author of *Common Sense for the Healing Arts*

Masterful acupuncturist Dianne Connelly has written a paean to healthy living. But the book is less about health than about wisdom. With her own definitions and explications of essential words to live by, with poetry such as filled her previous book, *All Sickness Is Homesickness,* and with personal stories from her own life and the lives of those she has treated, Dianne points the way to a life of spirit and courage.

– GUY HOLLYDAY, PHD, MAc

Environmentalist, practitioner of Acupuncture and Zero Balancing

Mentor, soul-hearted medicine woman and teacher Dianne Connelly offers her beloved readers the gifts of awakening to a gentler world, singing new possibilities for oneness one word at a time.

– BRIGITTE MANEKIN

Friend, Mother and Grandmother

Dianne Connelly — known for her keen eye for distinctive, inspirational words, for her energy and her inventiveness — in *Medicine Words* invites involvement with and love for each other and the planet. *Medicine Words* supports the reader in making powerful new shifts in thinking about our language, in using it with each other and in viewing it as an act of creation.

– BETSEY HEUISLER

Artist and teacher

Dianne masterfully reminds us that with each word we choose we create heaven or hell for ourselves and others.
— SUSAN DUGGAN, MAc
Acupuncture practitioner and massage therapist

When I imagine what it means to live authentically one's full essence, sharing unconditionally and abundantly, I think of Dianne Connelly and her book. Thank you, Dianne, for this great book, a heart-filled blessing.
— OLGA DEBAKEY
Beloved daughter of Katrin and Michael DeBakey

Medicine Words

Also by Dianne M. Connelly

Traditional Acupuncture: The Law of the Five Elements
All Sickness is Home Sickness
Alive and Awake: Wisdom for Kids
(with Katherine Hancock)

Many of the essays in *Medicine Words* appeared originally in *Meridians,*
a periodical published by Tai Sophia Institute.

Medicine Words

Language of Love for the
Treatment Room of Life

Essays by Dianne M. Connelly, PhD

Tai Sophia Press

Dedication

To all grandmothers and grandfathers—
the elders who know that the words they live
create the discourses for the children.

To Mary Ellen Zorbaugh, a grandmother
who lives knowing that a language of love is
the best medicine for the next generations.

Table of Contents

Acknowledgments

What is a language of love? With what words, with what sounds on breath do I make meaning, do I create a world? What I call "medicine words" are words that have helped me live, helped shape my life—the logos of my being. They are personal, though not private. Here, I note words that have given me life, and acknowledge the beloveds who have shared them.

"Our" Mama.* These words I heard often throughout my lifetime with Mama: "Dianne, life is short; kiss it, and kiss it now. Life is full of holy bumps; they all need to be kissed."

Mama's version of "oneness": "We all look alike on the john."

"Our" Pa. Words said by Pa on the farm in northern New York: "You can't pre-poop the cows, Dianne. When they poop is when you muck 'em.'"

More words from Pa: "Life is not a one-walk dog. You can't take that dog on one long walk and think you're done. That dog's going to need at least one walk every day."

---

* My Mama Irene is "our" mother through me. At Tai Sophia, we recognize each of us as an expression of the whole: I-you-he-she-we.

Pa's words on the death of our Mama Irene, spoken to all six of her children: "My Irene-y is solid in God's pocket."

"Our" Monsignor Joseph Luker. Words the Monsignor said to me in the orphanage: "Little girl, you look me in the eye. You are as good as anybody."

"Our" Midwife, Chloe. Words spoken during the birth of my son, Blaize, as Chloe took my hand to her breast and looked me in the eye: "Dianne, you know how to do this. Now do it."

"Our" Grandson, Tamar. Words from Tamar when he saw a picture of Sadie (my great friend), who had died: "Who died her? Who died Sadie?"

These speakings call me to love more, to open my listening, to make room for all of being—for all beings side-by-side-by-side. I am grateful for these "worders" who have spoken to me their language of love.

Overture

Beloved, in this chapter, the overture for this book, I choose the word "beloved" to address you—whoever you are. Millions of years are reflected in this moment of language between us Our world worded together, we belong to each other. As you read what I have written, you grant me being. This is Dianne writing—a holy particular from the great oneness of being; this is you reading—a holy particular from the great oneness of being. I call you beloved in the same way the Dalai Lama says there is no such thing as a stranger, only a friend we haven't met as yet.

I am reminded of Nina, a young woman in a workshop I was doing in New York. To everyone there, to 60 fellow two-leggeds, Nina blurted out, "I'm in love with youse guys!" It was only 20 minutes into the workshop and no one "knew" anyone else, yet every one of us nodded, concurring. In each other's presence, we wake up to being here together.

What words will I use to language this mutual presence, this being together? Being and loving are the same word. Heidegger said that our forgetfulness of being is in our speaking. The Sufi say the first word is "Ah," and all the rest are meant to be forms of that deep awe of being at all. As I wake up to speaking as a shining on being here with each other — a recollection that we are here — then, like a violinist using the bow on her violin, I call to you, beloved, in a language of love, to loving each other into being through our words.

Although the Tao is the Tao that cannot be spoken, I am ever awakening to language as a complex, fundamental phenomenon of our being together to establish a world, to make meaning and share the meaning, to put sound on this gift of breath—this gift that we cannot earn, and that is not owed to us. With this breath we breathe life into one another; we get so close to the unspeakable that every word emerges as an "Ah," a gift, a shining on being here at all, a love song, a medicine word.

By "medicine" I mean anything that helps us to be at peace and at ease in our daily breath. The words I have chosen so far for this writing build a world of welcome, a world of being side by side, dwelling together. Life is not a parking lot, nor is it a pathology. The old song, "Side by Side," comes to mind. Sing it now if you know it: "Oh, we ain't got a barrel of money, maybe we're ragged and funny, but we'll travel along, singing a song, side by side. Through all kinds of weather, what if the sky should fall? Just as long as we're together, it really doesn't matter at all… 'cause we travel along, singing a song, side by side."

Rhymes and songs and poetry are good medicine …"How beautiful thou art to me, my love, how beautiful thou art…" (Solomon in the Song of Songs). Singing to one another the great love poetry moves us toward a language of love, helping us to know our beauty and goodness and worthiness day by day.

Our medicine for one another is our very life; all the ways life has lived us belong, through us, to the whole. Nina's words, "I'm in love with youse guys," are fingers pointing to the moon of being, of loving—and wording that love.

In all the chapters of this, "our" book (it is ours now, as you hold me in your hands), it is my intention to unconceal language as an ongoing gift of love for the treatment room of our being together, our living room, our breathing time. The world I am designing with you is word by word by word. Everything we say is something about being, something about bringing forth our life together.

This "overture" is to create an opening through word that makes apparent the beauty and range of the great symphony of being — every word a gift, a giving thanks, a new possibility, an offering to the listener/reader.

Every word is formed by someone, some holy particular, some unique living, breathing, bodying-forth being saying something about being here…

> Words lead to deeds.…they prepare the soul, make it ready,
> And move it to tenderness.…
> *Saint Teresa of Avila*

In the beginning was the Word, and the Word was with God,
And Word was God.
John 1:1

You could not find the end of the soul though you traveled
everywhere, so deep is its logos.
Heraclitus

The first word, "Ah," blossoms into all others....
Kukai

One word frees us of all the weight and pain of life.
That word is love.
Sophocles

So is a word better than a gift.
The Apocrypha

One word determines the whole world.
Zen saying

The meaning of a word is its use in the language.
Ludwig Wittgenstein

PART I

Choose a Word,
Create a World

With Words
We Open Life — Or Close It

Oh for a word,
one phrase in which to fling
all that I think and feel,
and so to wake the world . . .
Fernando Pessoa

A WORD is dead
When it is said,
Some say.
I say it just
Begins to live
That day.
Emily Dickinson

Gradually, I'm changing to a word . . .
Stanley Kunitz

Our forgetfulness of being
is in our speaking.
Martin Heidegger

Everything said is said by someone.
Umberto Maturana

Listen to the word the way
a child listens to the sea
in a seashell.
Gaston Bachelard

What we say matters to the mood and movement of daily action. A simple, mundane example is a bumper sticker saying, "Life's a bitch and then you die!" and a bumper sticker saying, "Life's a gift, so live in gratitude." These are two different texts, two different speakings, two different conversations.

We are the speaking beings making the world in conversation, every word a correspondence in the world, a part of the text.

Welcome to this conversation. According to *Onion's Etymological Dictionary,* "to converse" is to dwell, to keep company with, to pass on one's life, to exchange words, to turn with—*con* (together) and *vertere* (to turn)—to turn together, to speak life together.

In being speakers for life, I assert that you and I, dear reader, forget the privilege and power of conversation, of speaking life and thus making new listenings for our tribe. We forget the power speaking has in the body, our vessel, our container for being. As we converse, we make up the text of our village, the texture for the life of us living, embodied villagers.

As beings of the human sort dwelling in language, we need especially now to regard seriously and rigorously what needs to be spoken—what wants to be spoken—what conversations are big enough for creation. It's not okay to say just any old thing about anything. Speaking is a moment of birth, an act of creation. Words are like the grapes of the vineyard—they make up the text, the taste, the quality, the color, and the sounds of the journey.

We experience life as we interpret it, as we speak it.

What is the text I speak? What distinctions do I make to you? What speaking would turn us newly together for a new conversation? Though it might sound awkward and unusual, what speaking would make a new listener of you, a new observer giving new possibilities to the experiencing?

Allow me to give you an example. I fell and broke my wrist in the days I have been writing this piece. How else could I say this? What would it matter if I said, "In the dance of heaven and earth, I have been asked to learn some new steps, to make some new movements, and develop new thinking, new actions." What if I say, "I fell and touched the earth harder than usual and now have a new sense of body and the poetry of limbs."

What if I say, "the work of healing this brokenness is the work of the world for all brokenness." Whatever I say becomes an invitation to turn together, to converse, to open life, or close it.

The power of the university, the press, the pulpit, is the power to share and create the world, i.e., the power to speak and listen, the power of language, of being in conversation—the power to move creation into life. What we say matters to the listener. Cicero knew speaking as an act of creation with his audience.

First is *that* we interpret, second is *what* we interpret—if we reveal *that* we do, then we can freely, spontaneously, examine our interpretations, making new ones, moving old ones out of certitude back into inquiry. We can use our speaking to grant being and open new listening for existence, words for new possibilities of world.

P. S. I intend these "conversation" entries to become an ongoing remembering that words are our needles, i.e., our instruments of peace, passion, possibility, wherever we are on planet earth, not just the treatment room—every room—bedroom, boardroom, classroom . . .

On Seeing the Saint...

At the bottom of each word,
I'm a spectator at my birth...
Alain Bousquet

When the pickpocket sees the saint on the road, all the pickpocket sees is the saint's pockets." So, I ask myself—and you, as you read and therefore ask with me—what are my "pickpocket conversations"? What is the possibility of seeing the saint?

As an acupuncture practitioner in the treatment room, I have learned to use the needle as an opening to life for another, the needle as a call to the saint—the holy whole of the other, including all the phenomena, all the "showing," all the constellation of existence, including what we have come to name "disease." To see only "disease" is to be picking the pocket!

I assert that our experience of being alive is largely determined by what we are saying about being alive, moment by moment, event by event, symptom by symptom, day by day. It lives in our conversations with ourselves, because how I interact, how I act, follows from what I interpret to be so. Disease, like any phenomenon that we name, lives in conversation. The conversation directs what we do. What I deem something to "be" determines what I "do" with it.

Thus, disease lives not just in the body but also in the interpretation each patient makes of the disease, that is, in her lived suffering. And the conversation between the person and her practitioner, i.e., guide, coach, friend,[1] can be a crucial, sometimes even *the* crucial constituent in the way a person interprets her disease — therefore, in her existential suffering.

When my patient Charlotte (see "Hymn to Charlotte" in *All Sickness is Homesickness*)[2] came to me having been diagnosed, i.e., "named" with a disease "cancer," she asked that I be with her through to her death, and that I not lose sight of her at any moment along the way. In other words, she asked me to be the observer for the saint, the observer for the holiness of her, for the possibility of her life and death, including all of the phenomena of her existence, all the "showing" of her.

Essentially, Charlotte asked me to recognize and go beyond my own "pickpocket" conversations about death so I could be in the presence of awe with *her*. She needed me to see more than just her pockets! Together, we kept in view the magnificence that was Charlotte; and even as she was dying, she healed, and she healed others.

To a practitioner for life, which I assert we all are, these questions about how we interpret the phenomena of life are crucial ones. As we take down the treatment room walls and seriously enter all the rooms of being alive — not just the treatment room where we use a needle — what begins to show is that we must "be" the needle, the presence for the possibility of the other, wherever we are, no matter what.

In these "conversation" pieces, I intend to build a dwelling–thinking with you (*vertere*, turn; *con*, with) such that there be a little new opening for us to "live into" together, a little new movement that shows the poetry of existence, a little new speaking and listening for the possibility of being alive.

Thank you for your friendship in these "turnings" together.

Life is not a finished action…
Teilhard de Chardin

NOTES
1. I would use the word "doctor" here if we had a new "listening" for this word that derives from the root *docere*, "to teach"; for now, though, I prefer the other words — guide, coach, friend.

2. Dianne M. Connelly, *All Sickness Is Homesickness,* 2nd edition. Laurel, Maryland: Tai Sophia Institute, 1993, pp. 139-41.

From Addiction to Benediction— "Word Be Born"

> Words are with us everywhere... We're often no more aware of them than our own spit, although we use them oftener than our legs.
>
> *William Gass*

Acupuncture and addiction are in the media as go-togethers these days. I've been thinking about that, and especially about the coercive power of that word "addiction."

The world called forth by the word "addiction" is a world of badness and problems, heartaches and headaches, crimes and vices, violence and sorrows, diminishment and imprisonment, of suffering humanity. That word-world holds no hope, no possibilities. Yet according to my etymological dictionaries, addiction might actually be about possibilities. Its Latin root, *dicere*, means "to say," and we humans are the sayers, the ones who "addict," who speak habitually against (*ad*) or toward (also *ad*) some facet of existence: We are the ones who "say" what life is.

Then I thought about the word "benediction," and how close it is to "addiction" through their common Latin root. The words are not far apart, yet the world called forth by the word benediction rarely crosses over into the world of addiction. Benediction speaks of *bene*, of goodness and blessings, of gifts and promises, of holiness and homing, of mercy, godliness, virtues, and caring humanity.

Humans are the sayers for the well of being, speakers of the *bene*, calling forth the blessedness of existence. We *say* who we are and who others are, and then we act accordingly. In this way we all are dictators. We dictate what it is to "be" in the "be" of human being. We are "addictators" and "benedictators"; we create life by our speaking it, blessed or hopeless.

At the Baltimore Detention Center for women, in a program for so-called "addicts," Tanya, an 18-year-old mother of three, and 42-year-old Francine, a woman with "no place to go but back to the streets," meet face-to-face daily with Peter, age 45, Greek descendant and acupuncture practitioner, and with Clemency, age 35, an Annapolis resident and student of acupuncture.

What do we *say* about what they and others in the program are doing there? I say that together they are bringing the world "benediction" to the world "addiction." Together they are bearing the sorrows of life; together blessing the bearing; together making offerings — each a unique gift — for all the rest; together learning life, each through the others.

After talk and treatment, Francine says, "I feel more peaceful now, naturally high, more rested." "Does it match the seduction of the drugs?" asks Peter. "No, not yet, but I think it could," she says. "And before, I didn't think anything could. The kids on the street say 'word be born' when they agree that something can be done. *Word be born, Peter.*"

Do we know that we put a face on humanity by our every word? O word-makers, do we take seriously the making of the world, our dwelling together here face-to-face, each of us an addict and each of us a benedict, each of us speaking life from what we have learned so far? O world-makers, do we take seriously the making of the word?

Our human conversations give us our human face. I venture that from a God's-eye view that face is godly, a benediction amidst all our addiction — if we are willing to word the world as blessing, and to give our lives to one another.

Killer Narrative

Because every day they chop heads off
I'm silent.
In each person's head they chopped off
was a tongue,
for each tongue they silence
a word in my mouth
unsays itself....[1]
Denise Levertov
"Thinking About El Salvador"

Recently I saw the movie about the holocaust, *Schindler's List.* The holocaust is an unspeakable horror of actions based on a conversation spoken by and agreed upon by specific human beings—a killer narrative. No nepenthe, no soothing syrup can remove the suffering inflicted by a killer narrative, a conversation that results in extermination. Among the dying cries and silences we can almost not see or hear that what happened was a discourse—a speaking and listening, a conversation inciting and perpetrating annihilation.

In the heart of those horrifying atrocities stood a man named Schindler, who constructed a different discourse, risking his life to save life, playing the system to fool the system. His was a heroic speaking and listening of life. At one moment by acknowledging the humanity of the SS guards in his factory, he disarmed them as adversary. At another moment he requested a three-minute silence from everyone in memory for all who "have died in these cruel years." Schindler's narrative about life was big enough to stand like a strong tree in a horrendous prevailing wind, big enough to end some suffering, big enough to show forth human goodness. Inscribed on a gold ring made and given to him by the Jewish prisoners was this statement in Hebrew: "He who saves a single life saves the world entire."

Now I come to today's "news"—and it does not even matter which day it is that "today" refers to, for actions from killer narratives are daily fare: "Man dies of beating," "High-powered bullets kill officer," "17-year-old boy slain"—drugs, proliferation of guns, poverty, discrimination, disintegrating families, the leading motive for homicide simply stated as "arguments." And, these are only the local headlines; national and international news describe variations of these annihilating actions.

You and I are of the same human race as Adolf Hitler and Mother Teresa. Taking the Tao seriously, we *are* one. The killer narratives are mine and yours. The killings are ours. Part of *us* pulls the trigger, not simply "those people out there." Our own triggered listening and speaking beget the murderous actions—conversations too small to show forth the wonder and possibility of existence.

How do we read of yet another perpetration, "Three more killed in drive-by gunfire," and just read on without pondering: What listening of life will I have today? What speaking? What discourse will be big enough to offer different possibilities, result in other actions? Will we, like Schindler, risk what we call "our lives," and in some strange virtuous ways, some extraordinary acknowledgments, some uncommon sense, some unaccustomed calls for silence, create new narratives wise and noble enough for us human beings to live goodness—one specific human being to another? Will I face my cruel, constricting narratives? Will I, this very day, plunk down every thought, word, and action toward serving our children and honoring our ancestors? Will you?

Let us practice these questions, this inquiry.

Let us practice "Yes."

NOTES
1. Denise Levertov, excerpt from "Thinking About El Salvador" in *Oblique Prayers: New Poems with 14 Translations from Jean Joubert* (New York: New Directions, 1984), p. 33.

In Our Conversations, Incarnations

For it is the world that speaks in us
And we are the world that we have to sing
The air will snatch whatever we love
Unless we hide it in our mouths
By speaking it quaintly as it comes
To say now what informs our lives…
William Stafford

We, beings of the human sort, are languaging beings. We live in language. Our joys and sorrows and glories live in language. All our concerns are held in conversation—someone speaks, someone else listens, and a world is born between us. As more join the conversation, a world is born among us. Then, we live in these worlds, not as invented discourse generated by our conversations, but as "the way it is," truths and certainties.

We forget that we are the generators of the conversations, and that they are no more and no less than our speakings and listenings. It could even be said that we are always only a conversation away from a new world of possibility. If we observe that we originate the conversations in the first place, that very observation becomes ground to create a fresh "turning together" (from the root of "conversation," *con-vertere,* turning with).

Allow me to use an example here, about a conversation that goes by the name "education." It houses a world of concern about what human beings call learning, knowing, information, data, acquisition of knowledge, enlightenment, intelligence, memorizing, remembering, studying, reading, being learned, schooling, credentialing. To go with the concern, we have generated departments of education; we have made developmental education; we have made systems of education; we have made principles, methods, and trainings; we have made databases on education. We have schools of all sorts. Education has become an "is," a certainty, a truth that everyone must have some of, a commodity, a thing; and in many instances we have made "it" a god, separate from living.

Speaking of the certainties around "education," my 17-year-old daughter, Jade, is in Bremen, Germany, as I write this to you. She quit senior year of high school to go live with our friends Ivan Illich, Barbara Duden, and Lee Hoinacki in their household of hospitality and conversation.[1]

This is what Jade told me of a conversation she had with Ivan one day:

Jade said, "Ivan, I'm learning so much being here with you."

He said, "You only think that because you have been schooled to think you are learning."

She, a bit shocked and discomfited, said, "Well, Ivan, if I'm not learning, what am I doing?"

"Jade," he said, "you are living."

With those few words, Ivan directed the conversation about "learning" to the phenomena of life. He helped Jade see "learning" in the dailiness of living—in *her* living—not, as culture speaks of it, as a body of knowledge that one "attains."

And, in that exchange, Ivan listened and responded with exquisite sensitivity to the phenomena of Jade's life.

We have fallen asleep to our very privilege of speaking and listening together. And we have made a deity of a conversation that now we must bow to, legally and socially, sometimes blatantly, sometimes less obviously. What are we obscuring, even obliterating by so doing? Simply said, we are obscuring life—distancing ourselves from our own being, distancing ourselves from others.

As speaker and listener we have disconnected from the phenomena of our lives. We have become invisible, unhearable, untouchable, unfleshed, dead in a system, disembodied from the very lips and ears, hands and eyes of one another who built the conversation in the first place.

My ear belongs to your word, your eye belongs to my writing hand. This moment when one mouth, a word, an ear live together—this is the moment of origin. We spring from the senses of one another...we are the seedboxes of each other's beginnings. All human endeavor and concern live there between and among us in language, that incarnation of our senses. We incarnate domains, then act in these domains without seeing, hearing, feeling, smelling, tasting, touching the unique phenomena of the speaker and listener who designed those domains.

Our concerns belong to each other as living breathing speaking listening. We now house these concerns in conversations about certainties—certainties like that we call "medicine" around a concern for body, "religion" around a concern for meaning, "law" around a concern for justice, "housing" around a concern for shelter, "money" around a concern for exchange, "work" around a concern for livelihood. The concerns come from the phenomena of being alive. The certainties come from conclusions that obscure the concerns—even erase concerns. Hence we view our concerns as certainties rather than see them with ongoing wonder, as the phenomena of our life here together.

So, I end this note to you, dear reader. And lest we forget, this writing is also a conversation, another turning together, another moment. Thank you for listening to this speaking. My writing hand belongs to your eye, my lips to your ear.

NOTES
1. See *Utne Reader,* January-February 1995, for Ivan Illich's thinking; for Lee Hoinacki's, see *Utne Reader,* March-April 1995.

"Yoohoos" from the Soul

In the summer I turned seven, I climbed a ladder that was leaning against my house. I recollect falling from the ladder and landing on my back, experiencing what I would later learn to call "getting the wind knocked out of me." I remember looking up to see the faces of my mother and father above me, and from that view thinking, "I am going to die." For the first time, I knew I was alive. I became aware that I am, and aware that I know that I am. This was my first recollection of *being*. And with this waking to being came a profound unknowing wonder: Could I ever not be? What is it to die? What is the difference between life and death, alive and dead?

I've since learned that I had experienced a moment of "anamnesis," a word that has begun to dwell in my inquiry about the phenomenon of being alive. I first heard the word from Ivan Illich, in conversation. Later I found that Plato, giving voice to Socrates, refers to anamnesis in the dialogues *Phaedo* and *Meno*. Anamnesis can translate as "recollection." It conveys the notion that living is an ongoing act of recovering from forgetfulness (amnesia), of remembering who we are, of raising existence to consciousness. It calls us to become observers of the phenomenon of being alive. For Plato this call comes from the soul—a kind of "yoohoo" to the Good, the Beautiful, the Just, the Holy.

Anamnesis is not exactly remembering, not reconstructing an incident from the past. It is not "taking a history," not a narrative of the rearview mirror. Anamnesis is being in the present, recollecting some instance in living where I became conscious that I am conscious—a moment when reflection, contemplation, wondering, or inquiry inspired a "coming to," a waking up.

Anamnesis does not live in the clock time of the past or the future. It does not live in space. Anamnesis exists embodied everywhere all the time, moment by moment. It is simply the becoming aware that we are wherever we are in this moment, and that what I am recollecting is the Beautiful, the Just, the Good and the Holy that we belong to, that belongs to us.

So what does "anamnesis" have to do with us here—acupuncturists, patients, readers? Well, it points to what we're about as beings of the human sort: We are not here to diagnose one another, that is, not here to determine categories of "wrongness" and then prescribe how to "fix" those labeled ills. Rather, in being with each other, we remember who we are: With you, I come to know myself as beautiful and good; with me, you recollect your goodness and beauty.

In each other's presence, in our conversations, our turnings together, we call each other to inquire together, to bring our senses present to everything so we may recover from our forgetting and recollect our "soul."

SAINT FRANCIS AND THE SOW
The bud
stands for all things,
even for those things that don't flower,
for everything flowers, from within, of self-blessing;
though sometimes it is necessary
to reteach a thing its loveliness,
to put a hand on its brow
of the flower
and retell it in words and in touch
it is lovely
until it flowers again from within, of self-blessing;
as Saint Francis
put his hand on the creased forehead
of the sow, and told her in words and in touch
blessings of earth on the sow, and the sow
began remembering all down her thick length,
from the earthen snout all the way
through the fodder and slops to the spiritual curl of the tail,

from the hard spininess spiked out from the spine
down through the great broken heart
to the blue milken dreaminess spurting and shuddering
from the fourteen teats into the fourteen mouths sucking and
blowing beneath them:
the long, perfect loveliness of sow.[1]
Galway Kinnell

In this poem, St. Francis calls the sow to being to remember, to recollect herself—her long, perfect loveliness. This is a call to consciousness, here, in the moment, exactly as we are. This is anamnesis.

NOTES
1. "Saint Francis and the Sow" from *Mortal Acts, Mortal Words* by Galway Kinnell. Copyright (c) 1980, renewed 2009 by Galway Kinnell. Reprinted by permission of Houghton Mifflin Harcourt Publishing Company. All rights reserved.

Speaking as a Gift

Everything said is said by someone.
Umberto Maturana

In the last essay I wrote of anamnesis—a recovering from amnesia. A waking up to being alive. This piece follows on from that one. It is a remembering of a call to awakening, to wakefulness.

"You look me in the eye," he said. "You are as good as anybody." I was nine years old. He was 50. His name was Joseph Luker. I knew him as Monsignor. It was when I was in the orphanage after my dad's death. My mother, in an astounding act of courage, split up her family of six children for one year so she could go to beauticians' school and learn a skill to earn a living for us all. My brother and I went to the St. Joseph's Orphanage.

Monsignor became my friend, my counsel, my practitioner. He didn't use needles, he simply used his senses. He saw my downcast eyes and my shoulders hunched forward. He listened to my barely audible voice and heard the assessment of the nuns who concluded that I was "painfully shy."

Then he spoke, and by speaking called me in my girlhood to a new awakening, a new possibility beyond what I already knew. "You look people in the eye. You are as good as anybody." He gave me the charge of answering the telephone and the doorbell, greeting whoever came to visit. It required me to practice looking others in the eye. He instructed me to walk up and down stairs with a book on my head. And with that practice I learned to hold myself upright, to move through life with a confident posture. It was an awakening in my child's body, a new possibility, a new conversation in which to dance life.

His spoken word was truly his needle, his gift. In the presence of this great gift, this action of love in language, I opened to a whole new way of being. Monsignor offered me a conversation and a new narrative of being alive in exchange for my old narrative, a story that was clearly too small to live in, a conclusion in which I, as a little girl, was suffering needlessly.

He was an observer—not in the question "What is wrong with Dianne? How can I fix her?" He was observer in the inquiry "What is the possibility for her? How can I assist her in creating a new opening?" These are two fundamentally different ways of looking at life. The speaking and listening that come from them are very different. In one, I am a problem. In the other, I am a new possibility. Like Monsignor, we get to choose how we see life around us.

As observer for possibility, Monsignor Joseph offered me another view, and he gave me very specific ways to practice this new way of being that would help me embody the good he saw. "You are as good as anybody. Look people in the eye."

What if he hadn't spoken? What if he had withheld his observings, his offerings, his calling me to practice? It isn't that he owed it to me, or that I could earn it from him. He spoke. I listened. The world opened, is still opening all these years later. That speaking—that treatment—became a turning point in my life. And in turn, Monsignor's gift to me becomes an offering I make to others. In my presence I intend that those I am with—the waitress, the seminar participant, the person lying on the treatment room table—know themselves as good and worthy.

Reader, what I ask you to receive is this: You are speaker. You give voice to life. You give life a voice. What you speak matters to the listener. Every speaking is a treatment, an act of creation. When one human being speaks and another listens, a world is born—a conversation that makes new actions possible.

For whom are you the Monsignor? What are you saying to the child you put to bed at night, to the person by your side, to those in life with you? We are Joseph Luker to each other. The question is, how wakeful am I—are you—to speaking as an act of creation? Are we taking it on? When my son's teacher thoughtlessly spoke to a student in class, "Don't go back there and sit with the losers," he gave voice to life in a way that resulted in tremendous unnecessary suffering. He spoke, and life shut down in the children in his classroom. The teacher was not wakeful to his speaking as an offering, a gift, an act of creation.

So when you are with another, call her, him, them, to their beauty and goodness. Offer them a practice they can embody. Let your speaking be a gift.

PART II

A Dictionary for Life

Observing Together — A Sacred Activity

Let's write a dictionary, reader. Let's gather some words, create interpretations, and so build—and rebuild—our world. We beings of the human sort possess this gift: We create the world with our words. Our daily actions are shaped by the words we use to language our experience.

I recommend that "observer" be the first word to which we give meaning. For the moment, I'll write and you read—however, do not forget that in your reading we are building together. With our pondering we will define a new world in this word.

Let us define "observer" as *she who is awake*. Observer:

She who sees that she sees.

She who has awakened to awareness that she is awake.

She who recognizes herself to be in practice, engaged in ongoing awakening, noticing, noting, "nota bene"-ing.

She who knowingly draws distinctions in language for the sake of life around her.

She who distinguishes and separates the phenomena she witnesses from the story she puts together about the phenomena.

She who recognizes herself as a speaker for remembering being. (Heidegger wrote that our forgetfulness of being is in our speaking.)

She who regards, is thoughtful.

She who considers, contemplates.

She who practices being awake to life as phenomena and listens long and deep.

She who speaks, aware that she is speaking.

She who builds the world with the listener, aware if the listener is learning to know who she (the listener) is by being with the observer.

She who bows to life as a phenomenon exactly as it is.

She who beholds this day in creation.

She who hallows the moment by her awareness.

She who recognizes that she is never describing objective reality—rather, she is describing the phenomenon exactly as she sees it, no more, no less.

She who celebrates being in the dance, even with its stumbles.

She who opens her eyes to the fact that she has eyes.

She who knows she does not know.

She whose wakefulness is a wake-up call to those around her.

She who is in awe that we are here at all and that we are here together.

She who is aware of being embodied, enfleshed—aware of the "bodyhood" in which all of life happens.

She who takes awareness seriously, as sacred.

She who recognizes herself making meaning, interpretations.

She who is in daily practice to keep the senses open for living, to recover from a senseless world.

She who is in practice to come to life more fully so as to serve life more wisely and more nobly.

So, reader, this first entry in our dictionary gives us ground for conversation, for taking seriously our making of language together. Now as I use the word "observer," you know what I mean. We have ground for our ongoing friendship, for building new, awake ways of being together. Before we die, we are bound to come to life together. Thoughtfully, respectfully, deeply listening, opening to new thinkings, speaking/listening the heart of us, we inquire together, an inquiry that might go something like this: What do you mean by that? Tell me your concerns, your learnings, your wisdom, your experience—teach me.

Remembering that a new vocabulary is a new world, let us be observers together in conversations current in our culture. Writing in a *Washington Post* editorial, William Raspberry told of a cab driver who used the word "sup" to mean "What's up?"—a way of saying hello. Yet the listener heard "sup" as an invitation to food. One word, two worlds. Will we train ourselves to be observers so as not to create opposition, so as to stay in inquiry about these worlds? Here the definition of "observer" becomes crucial.

We will create in these pages a dictionary of words/worlds to keep us awake to being, to build together ways of easing unnecessary suffering, ways of learning to bear what pain we must without adding to it—words/worlds to call us back from forgetting.

> I built a temple deep in their listening.
> *Rilke*

Awakening Life's "Ahh"

As I write, I observe, especially around the death of Princess Diana, our ever-present commentary—opinions, conclusions, interpretations, stories. Do we know that almost always in life we are commenting or allowing another to comment for us? What happens to a phenomenon in the presence of constant comment? Where does the wonder of "ahh" go? How can we keep our speaking as a living, breathing phenomenon, our every word in awe of life?

This piece, reader, is the next entry in the dictionary that we are compiling together. Our word is "phenomenon," and it closely follows "observer," our first entry. We defined an observer as one who is alive and who is awake to being alive and awake. In waking up, the observer sees the very existence of life as a phenomenon. As observers, each of us is a phenomenon observing life as a phenomenon.

What do we mean by the word "phenomenon"? We can define it as "what is manifest." And we also can say…

PHENOMENON:
- fundamental mystery of existence
- that which we can smell, hear, see, touch, taste
- something, not nothing
- what is given
- that which is the existence of something
- a revealing, an unconcealing

- what shows
- a particular of existence: "The class of elephants is not an elephant." (Bertrand Russell)
- something showing itself
- the thing itself
- that for which no "why" is required
- that for which no explanation is needed
- that which human beings "shepherd" through language
- that about which we tell a story, yet itself is not a story
- a living word: "The language is no longer lived, it is merely spoken." (George Steiner)
- a radiance, a shining
- a radiant word: "A word is not a crystal, transparent and unchanging. It is the skin of living thought."
  (Oliver Wendell Holmes)
- the "thatness" of being
- that which shows
- the unsayable for which we use words: "The first word, 'ahh,' blossoms into all the others." (Rumi)
- the "suchness" of a moment, a thing, a person
- the root of Divine showings, epiphany, diaphany, hierophany, theophany
- that in which Being can show
- a presence here and now
- that which is revealed, unconcealed
- the shared context of those who are alive and awake
- the practical happenings of everyday life, such as eating and sleeping
- awareness of the world
- the everydayness of things
- what is manifest

We are here together, dear reader, dancing with the mystery of being alive—and we dance our lives through language. We were born into language. Each of the 6.5 billion of us is living in at least one of the more than 5,000 languages of humankind. So, we find words, we make words, we repeat ready-made words. Each of these words has some moment of origin; it names a phenomenon, names one of life's showings, gives a meaning in which we have some say. We name the "thatness" which we perceive through our senses.

Now we see the importance of defining "phenomenon." We can use this distinction in the treatment-room-of-life, use it as we dance together in the mystery of our days and nights. I will know that you as a phenomenon are a "showing of life"—not my opinions, narratives, judgments, conclusions about you. You as "a particular of existence" do not exist as a replaceable part. You are not an abstraction. You are a flesh and blood showing of life, a being of the human sort whom I can smell, hear, see, touch and taste, and who lives in the "everydayness of things." You are not a generalization. You are a particular being perceivable through my senses. All I must do is open my ears and eyes and nose and mouth and skin to you. You are a being within reach of my senses, a being not to *diagnose* but to be *conscious* with.

There is a particular "thatness" about you, a "suchness," an unsayable "first word 'ahh'" about you. The here-and-now presence that you are is a land with so many stories—a storyland—and yet, you are not your stories, nor are you my stories about you. You are "a living radiant word" of Being itself, through which the "fundamental mystery of existence" shows. You are phenomenon. You are "life's showing of itself."

Can I, will I, allow you to be just exactly as you are? In my every interaction, my every conversation, will I practice opening to you as phenomenon, as Divine showing, or will I draw conclusions, tell stories, make commentaries too small to let you show as "a radiance, a shining"? This entry to our dictionary, reader, is a reminder that words are inseparable from what they name, and though we cannot speak "Being" itself, we can get very close.

> Somehow, the mystery of language was revealed to me. I knew then that w-a-t-e-r meant that wonderful cool something that was flowing over my hand. That living word awakened my soul, gave it light, hope, joy, set it free!…I left the well-house eager to learn. Everything had a name, and each name gave birth to a new thought….[1]
>
> *Helen Keller*

In the above passage from *The Story of My Life,* Helen Keller, deaf and blind, describes what happened as she worked with her teacher, Annie Sullivan, in the presence of the phenomenon "water." Day after day, Annie spelled words into Helen's hand, naming phenomena, giving her language.

NOTES

1. Excerpted from Helen Keller's autobiography, *The Story of My Life,* first published in 1903.

"That's One Way of Looking at It!"

In language we tell each other our lives. In words we are remembering ourselves. Every word stirs the life force. As observers we can speak the word in service of wisdom; we can create parables, stories that teach about the phenomena. For example:

My daughter Caeli said to me one morning, "I don't want to go to school—I have a tummyache. And besides, Mrs. Kerr is mean, Mommy. That's just the way she is." Caeli's suffering—her tummyache—was related to her conclusion about her teacher. I asked Caeli to go to school that day and find one thing she could say that was not "mean" about Mrs. Kerr. When Caeli came home from school, she did not mention her belly. When I asked what she noticed about Mrs. Kerr, she said, "I had fun in art class today. And Mommy, Mrs. Kerr has blue eyes like I do."

Our unnecessary suffering is in our conclusions. As Caeli unhooked her conclusion—"mean"—about her teacher, she had freedom to create art and even to enjoy being with her teacher. Her unnecessary suffering disappeared.

In the past few essays we have been creating a dictionary together. We've examined the words "observer" and "phenomenon." We defined observer as one who is awake to being alive and awake, and phenomenon as what manifests to our senses before we have a "story" about it—that which we can smell, hear, see, touch, and taste. In this essay we follow with the word "conclusion."

CONCLUSION:
- a naming of something, giving it a kind of "is-ness," as though I know fully what it is
- what a human beings says about a phenomenon. (For example, weather reporters can describe a rainy day as a phenomenon, or they can say it is an "unpleasant day" or that the weather is "bad"—conclusions about the phenomenon "rain.")
- saying something about existence
- a sentencing about being alive: "Life's a bitch and then you die," for example
- a diagnosis
- a construction about reality according to the someone who is speaking
- a turd from a "high cow": "It is so, I have spoken."
- a story regarding a phenomenon
- a narrative about a phenomenon
- a judgment on a phenomenon
- an opinion about a phenomenon
- someone says so, and someone listens and agrees or disagrees
- a report on a phenomenon
- a comment on a phenomenon
- a notion
- everyday decisions and closings and openings
- making an ending
- forming a final verdict or determination

Does a conclusion matter? I say that it does. We build the world together. If I speak something and you concur, we are naming something into existence.

Could I, could you spend one day, one hour, drawing no conclusions about anything, just remaining open with our senses to the phenomenon of being? In opening my senses to you, I may perceive that:
- I can hear you only faintly in the presence of my conclusion that "you *are* this."

- I can barely see *you* in the presence of my "stories," my conclusions *about* you.
- I can scarcely touch you because my stories are in the way.
- I can hardly savor the sweet goodness of you.
- I can capture merely a whiff of your wonder as I breathe.

We must become observers of our own conclusions, for if no observer is present, we are imprisoned by our conclusions, our diagnoses. However, when an observer is present, we can keep the conclusions distinct from the phenomena, and so we are free to form conclusions that have the power to serve life.

Conclusions are a necessity. The key is to be awake to them. Everything is a statement, a conclusion, a story made by someone about existence. The words you are reading at this very moment are my construction about life. The crucial question is, what do I say about being? And is it a conclusion big enough to serve the children and to honor the ancestors?

I assert that there are three certainties in life: that we are here (the phenomenon of existence); that we are here together (with each other—we are necessarily in relationship); and that we are mortal (the day will come when we are no longer here). The conclusions we make about these three phenomena will determine the peacefulness and possibility of our lives.

My dear friend and colleague, Julia Measures, one day called me to practice—as I now call you. I was walking down the hall at our acupuncture clinic, grumbling to myself. I was so caught in my own stew that I didn't see Julia at first. She observed my face, the way I walked, and as she passed by me she said, "Well, Connelly, that's one way of looking at it!" One simple sentence and I awoke anew to the phenomenon of being alive and to being a speaker for creation. Julia called me to notice that I was creating a story, some conclusion in which I was suffering unnecessarily.

I make an offering to you of a new practice: become very wakeful to conclusions. Practice nudging your narratives, opinions, judgments to the side. Practice saying, "Well, that's one way of looking at it!" when you observe yourself making up a story. Don't tell any story unless you intend it to be a teaching story that will serve the children and honor the ancestors. Have EVERYTHING you say be for the sake of life.

love's function is to fabricate unknownness

e.e. cummings

[35]

I Declare!

...Perhaps we are *here* in order to say: house,
bridge, fountain, gate, pitcher, fruit-tree, window—
...But to *say* them, you must understand,
oh to say them *more* intensely than the Things themselves
ever dreamed of existing....
Here is the time of the *sayable, here* is its homeland.
Speak and bear witness....[1]
Rilke

"Say it to be so" is not a puny ho-hum. Each speaking is the Tao according to someone—according to a once-in-all-the-world-never-to-be-repeated uniquely embodied speaker with a view. Each speaking is a perception of the Whole, a view of One from one—just as every wave is Ocean.

Each of us is saying something about Being, for the sake of the Whole, for the sake of each other. Through you, everyone you meet knows a bit more about who they are and the possibilities of life.

In these pages we have been compiling a dictionary, its purpose to redefine being alive together. Our dictionary word in this issue is "declaration," which naturally follows from words we've already defined: "observer," one who is alive and awake to being alive and awake; "phenomenon," that which manifests to our (the observer's) senses before we have a "story" about it: and "conclusion," the narrative, the things we say, the story we tell about what we see, hear, smell, taste, and touch.

So, alive and awake, what do I say? What do I declare about the phenomenon to which I have opened my senses? A declaration, I say, is not for the sake of itself.

"Declaration": that which is brought forth by a human being drawing a conclusion wakefully, as an offering, a gift.

Everything we say *must* be a gift—all speakings, when they are heard and built upon by others, become the "is-nesses" in which we live.

We dwell in conversations that house our shared cares, concerns, and declarations—declarations that become accepted as certainties and often go unexamined.

So, DECLARE:
- to have a "say"
- to choose an interpretation
- to be a speaker for creation
- to live as a listener of others' declarations
- to design every speaking as a gift, using words knowingly as action and offering
- to bring into being by speaking
- to assert, to make clear, to tell *(Skeat's Etymological Dictionary)*
- to announce the existence of (e.g., declaring war)
- to proclaim (e.g., Emancipation Proclamation)
- to act in the form of speech (e.g., in the Declaration of Independence: "We ordain and establish this to be so...")
- to create a text, a context for living
- to use language generatively (Ralph Waldo Emerson said, "I write only when I am inspired, and I see to it that I am inspired every morning by nine o'clock...." This is a declaration and a practice.)
- to say *nothing* that is not for the sake of life
- to recognize *silence*
- to declare—to bring into being by speaking

Speaking is never a disembodied action, even though the speaker may be invisible. Wherever words are used, someone is saying something—the Tao according to that unique speaker for creation. We need to stay awake to this: there is a speaker and, therefore, always an embodied point of view.

Further, we need to stay awake to what our speaking produces in another—something almost impossible to know unless, when speaking, we are aware *that* we are speaking, *what* we are speaking, and *how* we are building the word-world with others.

Phenomena come to life in the presence of our sensing bodies. Everything that appears I can define as disparate, diverse parts—I can speak of the world as a concluded set of objects. If, instead, I declare all the phenomena, all the perceived things to be ONE, to be integrally connected facets of a Whole, would it matter? (A first "bone"—that upon which everything else hinges—of Taoism is that all things are one in the unspeakable Tao.) When I interpret life as a seamless fabric of Oneness, do I take different actions, think different thoughts, create different moods?

Stephen's story illustrates the possibilities: Stephen, age 10, was present when I brought a loaf of bread to the SOPHIA for Kids program. Sitting together, everyone in the group looked at, touched, and smelled the bread, and told family stories about bread—the cornbread that Grandma made and Aunt Mary's biscuits. We thought about the gifts of nature in bread and how bread comes to be.

Each of us took a little hunk of the loaf. Before we tasted it, I asked, "Would it matter if we thought of this bread as many disconnected pieces or as one bread in many different places?" Then each child had his or her say about these two different ways of speaking about phenomena, about seeing separation or Oneness.

Later, Stephen told me about how he saw Oneness in his school—by his own say-so, his own declaration: "At lunch time I was eating a hamburger with a bun on it, and I looked over and saw this other kid eating a hamburger with a bun on it, and I thought, "We are eating bread together. The only thing is, he didn't know it. So I had to tell him." Stephen had taken his declaration to school with him. *Word be born.*

In speaking, we structure our very modes of thinking, of participating in creation. Our speaking and listening are ways in which we bring forth a world.

What are you saying to be so? Here are some declarations that I say serve: We are one in the dance of being alive, *and* we are here together for the sake of each other. We belong to each other, these eyes of mine designed for that face of yours— holy eyes, sacred face; these ears of mine for the sounds of you—loving ears, incarnate sound; these arms for your body—devoted arms, blessed body.

Nick, a young physician friend at the Mayo clinic, told me of Mary, a patient referred by a fellow physician. Mary suffered severe cramps, "crippling" by her own say-so. She was sure that something was wrong with her and that she was alone in her concern. Nick could hear Mary constructing a debilitating story of isolation around her pain. He also could hear that Mary was not an observer of herself as she storied the pain. To her, the pain and story were an "is," a declared "that is just the way it is, doctor."

Nick realized that he was constructing a different story around the phenomenon of Mary and her suffering. He didn't attempt to replace her story with this own, however. Instead, he asked Mary if she was willing, in partnership with him, to be a new observer of her body and a new observer of what she was saying about the pain. She said "yes." Within that declaration Nick and Mary together designed new speaking and new practices. Mary chose no longer to use the word "crippling" about her pain, and she chose to use her story about isolation as a teacher: when she heard herself telling that story, she used it to remind herself to breathe deeply and think of five other possible stories.

Mary also realized that how she is with her pain and suffering matters to her two young daughters, who are learning from her how to live. So, for their sake, too, she practices her new wakefulness. And Nick is getting requests from other doctors to teach them how to speak with their patients.

Oh, the lightness of being that lives in language, that lives in the declaration of possibility! Nick called Mary to the observer that she is of life as phenomenon, in the presence of which she can declare anything, from "something's wrong and needs to be fixed" to "something is possible, let's create it." She gets to choose life by declaration.

Word-world be born!

NOTES

1. From "The Ninth Elegy" by Rainer Maria Rilke, in *The Selected Poetry of Rainer Maria Rilke*, edited and translated by Stephen Mitchell (New York: Random House, 1982).

A Call to Practice

PRACTICE is the word we examine in this essay for the dictionary we are creating. You could say that our every action is a practice—brushing our teeth in the morning, putting on the kettle, doing the chores on the farm—actions that keep life humming along. The question is, are we *wakeful* to what we do? The Vietnamese monk Thich Nhat Hanh calls us in his writings to simple wakefulness to our every action, that is, to be in ongoing practice.

Practice comes with declaration. By declaration we say what practices are important, what we will be wakeful to throughout the day, and thus we design ways of being for our lives. For example, one of my patients, Anna, told me that she has designed a practice of doing whatever she does for the sake of her three nieces. So, when recently she was offered the drug of her former addiction, she thought of the little girls and said "no way." Anna, by declaration, has designed an effective practice to help her hold steady to a new way of being.

In another example, Ralph Waldo Emerson designed a practice to assure that his writing reflected what mattered deeply to him: "I only write when I'm inspired," he declared. "And I see to it that I'm inspired by nine o'clock every morning."

Practice is a lived, bodied action, and it requires wakefulness:

PRACTICE:
- application
- performance
- a habit of doing things
- to do
- an action, an act, a deed
- *agere,* to drive, to put into action

I was giving a workshop in San Francisco at the Delancy Street Foundation when I met Mary. She was showing me around the Foundation, which is a community of folks who live together, all of whom have been in prison, have been addicted to drugs, have committed crimes. And all have chosen to take on new practices. I was struck by Mary's friendliness and kindness and her ready smile. When I remarked on this, she said, "I realize my face doesn't belong to me. It is for your eyes and the eyes of all around me. And so what I do with it will matter to you. I've always been very good at scowling and being surly—I know how to do that very well. I am not so used to smiling and being kind and helpful, so I have taken that on as a new practice. When I forget, my friends remind me that I am in practice to smile and to be friendly."

Mary chose to practice joy. She made joy an embodied action, a brand-new learned way of being, because she declared that it matters.

When I lived in a Catholic girls' boarding school for my high school years, one of my teachers, Sister Mary William, called me to a specific discipline, a certain practice. Noticing how eager I was to read each letter I received from my mother, she asked that I not open the deeply desired letter for 24 hours. Thus she asked me to practice a "custody" of the eyes, training me to a kind of "ascesis." By this ascetic practice I learned to read my mother's letters in a holy and bow-filled way. I learned to take seriously where and on what I placed my eyes, and in what mode.

"Ascesis" raises questions for us: What if it is not okay to see or be shown just any old thing? What if the violence of our youngsters is a cry that we have no practice in nourishing the soul by what our eyes and ears take in?

When I describe the practice of curbing the curiosity of the eyes that sister Mary William taught me, some people consider it extreme self-denial for a young girl. Yet, as I look around at the world of my children, I observe a desperate need for practices in which the children become wakeful to their gifts, to their goodness, to their service, and to the gifts of others.

Enacting a new practice can be a struggle, and that is the way life is: when we were newly born we did not have the practice of walking, and no one could give it to us. Yet each of us took on the action "walking," cheered forward by our family. In the same way, we can give ourselves permission to be beginners in our practice. No one would ask beginning practitioners of walking to jog immediately after taking their first step, nor ask beginning practitioners of talking to recite a Shakespearean sonnet.

In this culture we tend to say something is "hard" or "difficult" when what we really mean is that we are not practiced at it. We have not yet cultivated a bodily sense of ease in that specific area of human endeavor. So every time you hear yourself say "this is hard," let that remind you to shift your speaking to "I am a beginner in this—I am not practiced in this particular area." Then observe whether you actually have more ease, ease that helps you learn whatever you must.

For those times when practice seems difficult, I offer you the words of my Pa, a farmer: "Dianne, life is not a one-walk dog. You can't walk that dog just one long time and think, 'There now, I've done it.'"

The world of the computer is a useful example for many of us who remember a time before the phenomenon "computer" existed and who found ourselves struggling in this new domain. I recall thinking, "This is hard, too difficult for me. I do not have the skill to learn this. Others can, but not me." In relation to "computer" I lost my observer and went into stories, old narratives and reactionary stews in which "computer" couldn't even show up as a possibility. I had made a conclusion and had no freedom to act effectively in relation to the word "computer." Only when I reconsidered my conclusion and gave myself permission to be a beginner did I take on the new practice of "computer."

In the same way, we can reconsider our conclusions—our stories—about "health." We can learn to shift our gaze from worrying about our health to cultivating the art of living and dying, of bearing what we must bear without adding unnecessary suffering. We can practice the art of being alive—for the everyday human challenge is to discern what serves life and to be wakeful to our actions. The challenge is to *practice*.

We Are All Beginners

I learn by going where I have to go.
Theodore Roethke

The word for our dictionary in this piece, dear reader, is "beginner." Here, we will use it as observers of life who are declaring new practices into existence. It's rather like a birthday as we celebrate the phenomenon that we are here, alive and awake in the great dance of being, and that we can learn new ways of being.

BEGINNER:
- she who enters into a new practice
- novice
- a person just beginning to do or learn something
- a person who is unskilled, inexperienced in some arena
- a person who is not yet free to act effectively in a new field
- a person who might say "this is hard" in the early stage of a new practice
- she who, in declaring herself as beginner, gets the joy and dignity of learning new ways of being

A beginner is one who declares herself to be in practice, who designs actions to become competent, who aims to act effectively and freely in some new way of being in which she is not yet practiced. In our last piece on "practice," we spoke of giving ourselves permission to be a beginner, that is, to take on a new facet of being alive that makes new actions possible. A beginner brings into being an aspect of what it is to be human in some particular domain of human concern—an embodied discourse, a practice, a new opening. A useful example here is the action of driving a car.

Cars were invented by human beings, and they were brought into existence from someone's idea, someone's thought of a new possibility. Before cars, there was the horse and carriage. Someone spoke, someone else listened, and through their words and actions coordinated the birth of the domain "horseless carriage" or "car."

Being a beginner at driving a car requires that I be an observer learning the distinctions agreed upon in the domain of "driving." Think back to the time before you had embodied the distinctions of driving. The brake, the accelerator, mirrors, ignition, speedometer, gas gauge, where to look, where to put the key, how to sit—they were all new to you. You were required to learn which actions to take under what circumstances, to coordinate your actions to prevent breakdowns, and not to create accidents. You learned to act in a peaceful way while driving—that is, to be at one with the actions of others in this domain of driving a car.

In our American culture, we get a learner's permit at age 15; it is permission to declare oneself a beginner. As beginners, we are not expected to know how to drive before we have intentionally taken on learning that skill, and have practiced with someone who embodies the distinctions of the domain. A person already in practice—a practitioner in the new domain—acts as our coach or mentor.

Each practice lives within a cultural context and a field of action. A beginner learns to recognize the domain of action she is acquiring and then learns to abide by its distinctions. When learning to drive, for example, we memorize the "rules of the road" and the way to operate the car; then we drive and drive until we've embodied those distinctions. During that time we may be tempted to say something like "Making a left-hand turn at an intersection is *hard*!" Eventually we achieve competence and have some freedom in the new arena. In the domain of car-driving, this stage is marked by our highly anticipated driving test.

As beginners, the seasons remind us of ongoing gifts and practices. Winter brings us into the unknown. The practice of being in unknowing, deep in the mystery of existence—the winter phase of the cycle—is a crucial steeping for all of us. Here in the unknown we are beginners. And we must learn Beginner's Mind, declaring ourselves beginners with all the dignity and joy of being brand new, approaching *this* day in creation as one that has never been before and never will be again. In this sense, we are all beginners together.

Lao Tzu said, "The ancient masters didn't try to educate the people, but kindly taught them not to know."[1] Stephen Mitchell, in this 1988 version of the *Tao Te Ching,* explains this passage: "The ancient masters taught them the supreme value of 'Don't-know Mind,' forever fresh, open, and fertile with possibilities. Another name for it is Beginner's Mind."[2]

Someone who is competent, that is, one who has the freedom to act effectively in a particular area, may not be competent in another, related matter. A person competent in the domain of driving a car, for example, may not be competent to tune it—that is a different action. There is tremendous freedom in recognizing and declaring that we are beginners in some domains, and also that we are competent, even virtuosos, in other areas. The permission to declare our competencies and to be a beginner is freedom. And we are all beginners in something.

I watch my daughter, Caeli, at age ten, going off to a new school. She says, "Mommy, I'm a little afraid."

"What do you mean, 'afraid'?" I ask her.

"I don't know what it will be like, what teacher I'll have, what friends will be in my class. I just don't know."

"Where in your body do you notice you're a bit tight, a bit squawky?"

"In my belly."

"What could you practice to be more at ease, honey?"

"I could sing that lullaby you sing to me at night, 'Tooralooraloora.'"

"Caeli, could you say that you are a beginner in being a sixth-grader? Whole new practices and possibilities?"

"Oh yes."

"And, Daughter, will you let yourself be a beginner and not think you should already know what you'll be learning today? As a beginner, will you stay open to whatever the day brings you?"

"Yes."

"Are you still afraid?"

"A little."

"What else are you, honey?"

"I'm excited, Mommy."

And off she went.

NOTES

1. Lao Tzu, *Tao Te Ching,* translated by Stephen Mitchell (New York: Harper & Row, 1988), No. 65.

2. Ibid., p. 104.

Word Word Word

We live in words. They pour down like rain all day long. We have our being in our speaking—and yet it is this very being that we forget in our speaking.

In the dictionary we're compiling together, dear reader, the word for this entry is "word." The only way to say anything about "word" is to use words. Words to speak "word." In words, the "word."

WORD:
- a phenomenon of sound on breath
- a unit of discourse
- a promise
- an embodied utterance
- a calling, telling
- a poetry of existence
- a declaration as "needle"
- a proverb, parable
- a pledge, offering, gift
- an epiphany
- a transport into the wordless
- a gift from the silence
- something said about being alive
- Logos, Love, God, Soul
- definition of our humanity
- lived meaning

The story goes that when Lao Tze was leaving China, a guard at the final gate asked the sage, "Old man, give us some words on the art of living." So the old man began by saying that the Tao itself cannot be spoken: "The tao that can be told is not the eternal Tao." Then he proceeded to write 5,000 words before he departed![1]

Although the "word" cannot be spoken, words point to the "word." Words are the gardening tools for cultivating the art of being alive, of bearing what we must, and in the end letting go of it all.

Hear poets and sages:

In the beginning was the Word, and the Word was with God,
and the Word was God.
John 1:1

You could not find the end of the soul though you traveled everywhere,
so deep is its logos.
Heraclitus

The first word "Ah," blossoms into all others...
Kukai

The word frees us of all the weight and pain of life.
That word is love.
Sophocles

So is a word better than a gift.
The Apocrypha

This word burned like a lamp.
The Apocrypha

Words lead to deeds....they prepare the soul, make it ready,
and move it to tenderness....
Saint Teresa of Avila

One word determines the whole world.
Zen saying

The meaning of a word is its use in the language.
Ludwig Wittgenstein

Words, after speech, reach into the silence.
T. S. Eliot

This word "love" which greybeards call divine.
William Shakespeare

The word of the earth in the ears of the world,
was it God? was it man?
A. C. Swinburne

Don't you boys be out there yellin' up somebody
'less you got somethin' they need to know.
Jim Autry

Gradually, I'm changing to a word.
Stanley Kunitz

The words in my mouth have gone dead,
and therefore self-destruction and dehumanization…
Eugene Ionesco

Life Grace Love — beautiful words to dwell on, these fall days.
Dorothy Day

Striving most gently to bring a fit word to everything.…
James Dickey

Lord, speak only the Word and my Soul shall be healed.…
The Holy Mass

Silence—this word also rustles across the page and parts the boughs
that have sprouted from the word "woods"…
Wislawa Szymborska

Could I embody…all that I bear, know…
breathe into one word…I would speak…
Lord Byron

Word Up! World be born!
Inner City Kids

Remember the dance
that language is,
that life is.
Remember.
Joy Harjo

I love Jesus, who said to us:
heaven and earth will pass away.
When heaven and earth have passed away,
my word will remain.
What was your word, Jesus?
Love? Forgiveness? Affection?
All your words were
one word: Wakeup.[2]
Antonio Machado

I have offered mostly quotes for this entry about "word," each of them said by someone, each pointing to what can't be said, each a gardening tool for cultivating life.

Each of us is a practitioner of word in our daily lived bodied existence. My intention is to "yoohoo" us to an awe of human language, so that every worded breath may be wakeful to the phenomenon of simply being. Our speakings are the words of our soul, our life, our breath—holy words, as Paul Celan observed in writing poetry after Auschwitz, using language of the devisers of Auschwitz.

What is the word on my lips now? Does it carry Goodness and Beauty for you? What word am I becoming as I live? And you, what word made flesh are you practicing?

At the hour of our death—when we realize our call has come and that it is time to go, time to leave all that we have known for the next great mystery of existence — what will be the last word on our lips?

Shall we create ourselves now as a love song? Shall we be in practice for our final word before the awesome silence of death? Shall we "ah" every word from now until then? Oh My Beloveds!

NOTES

1. Stephen Mitchell tells this story in his rendition of Lao Tzu's *Tao Te Ching* (New York: Harper & Row, 1988), pp. 85-86.

2. Antonio Machado, from *Proverbs and Tiny Songs,* translated by Robert Bly in *The Soul Is Here for Its Own Joy: Sacred Poems from Many Cultures,* edited by Robert Bly (Hopewell, New Jersey: Ecco Press, 1995), p. 248.

The One

Dear Reader, "observer,"* you who are alive and awake to the "phenomenon" of being alive and awake, my "practice" with you is to make a "declaration" with each writing of these "conversation" essays; to bring into being some "word" newly, to speak the word as a "beginner," thus redefining old conclusions we have made about being alive. We are still here, O My Beloveds, with the privilege and duty of wording creation, of creating the words from which to view being alive.

Here, together, we are creating a dictionary of such words. Each entry brings us to the treasure of listening and speaking, leading us to the mystery, the Great Silence, that lies within and beyond all words.

Our word for this time is "One."

ONE is:
- the irreducible, a seamless whole
- total being
- healing—knitting together what is apart, reconciling
- a circle—including All
- the Tao, the Way
- all of us
- integer, co-ordinate, being at one with
- in union with, nirvana, samadhi, sunyata
- universe

* Each word in quotation marks is studied in another entry.

- laughing with everyone, welcoming everyone and everything
- singular and limitless mystery of being
- unity of being

O My Beloveds, know the word as creation: "One," a verb, an action, a way of referring to each of us. We could say that there are 6.5 billion different human hearts beating in 6.5 billion different places. Or could we say (and would it matter if we say) one heart beating in 6.5 billion different places?

John Kabler, dear friend and patient, and head of Clean Water Action, practiced seeing oneness in all his actions. John recognized that all of us—whether the chief executive of an industrial company dumping waste, a housewife using detergents, or a student studying ecology—all of us need clean water. At John's funeral, we sang together "Row, Row, Row Your Boat" to honor his love and his vision of life-giving waters for us all.

Among the myriad manifestations of being, how shall we, beings of the human sort, perceive One? So many are we, so different in our colors and shapes and sounds and smells, tastes, and textures. We are so many different breads in the world—or what if we say we are One bread in all its humanity: communion? Yes, wakefulness to the word "One" calls the world to One, to our common union.

What is the language for One? How shall we speak One? A Tai Sophia student, Melanie, tells this story of her little brother Serge, age five: "One day in a store, Serge asked my mother, 'Mom, what does a stranger look like?' 'What do you mean, Serge?' 'Well, my teacher told me not to talk to strangers, so I want to know what one looks like.'" Serge saw only the One as he looked at other human beings. He was embodying Oneness until the moment he was called to see another as separate, as a "stranger."

In the Sufi tradition, Shams of Tabriz spoke of the One this way: "I, you, he, she, we—in the garden of mystic lovers, these are not true distinctions." Like little fish, ocean within and around us, we look for the ocean. Like the person in the Zen Oxherd pictures, we are sitting on the ox, looking for the ox.

One is our world. One is our starting place. One is our eternal return. One blue sky above us, around us. One great earth beneath our feet. One sun shining on us all. One ongoing breath of life, and then no more. One death for each of us. The ongoing news of this planet is that we are One, and we are One in our mortality. We are One in the unknown of when and how we die. We are One in the knowing that this moment will not happen twice.

The Vietnamese monk and teacher Thich Nhat Hanh bases all his teaching in the Oneness. He offers a practice to assist us in seeing that we are One with all others: Point your finger toward yourself with the thought, "I am pointing towards myself." Then, holding that thought, point your finger away from your body toward the phenomena around you: "I am pointing toward myself."

One is now. One is peace. Existence is a seamless whole. One. One shows itself in different forms—in the form of Two, of partnership, of Heaven and Earth, the dance of duality, birth and death, night and day, front and back, self and other, this and that. None of these exists without its partner; they define each other and are indivisible—One.

One shows itself in the form of Three—a breathing between the Two, between Heaven and Earth; a Two and their child, an arising from partnership, Life itself in the Ch'i of time, the hyphen in "I—Thou."

One moves as Four into the directions of space—the North, the South, the East, and the West, covering the whole.

One shows as Five—the dance of the Wu-Hsing, the movement of time and space in the four directions held by the Earth at the center; the Five of transformation, the ceaseless movement of One in its daily round.

And so we count by One, beginning from and returning to One, everything in life being an expression of and a manifestation of One. We do not stop breathing in order to see, nor stop singing in order to sit, nor stop sitting in order to smile, nor stop smiling in order for our blood to flow, nor stop thinking in order to keep our feet on the floor. We are an all-at-onceness—a seamless fabric of existence—One.

Redefining "Body"

Body my house
my horse my hound
what will I do
when you are fallen...

Where can I go
without my mount
all eager and quick
How will I know
in thicket ahead
is danger or treasure
when Body my good
bright dog is dead...[1]
May Swenson

Our word, dear reader, for this entry in the dictionary we're creating together is "body." It is a word embedded in the world as our very condition for being, yet a word little examined.

No one hears or writes the word, speaks the word, speaks or signs the word, who is not already in a body. None of us escapes concerns about being embodied; the nature of "body" is a permanent human concern. Aging, sickness and death continually call us to stay alive to ourselves as observers of what we have learned to call body. And yet, this very word lives in no single historical definition. Our view of "body" differs depending on the tribe into which we were born.

BODY:
- the somebody anybody nobody self (e.e. cummings)
- a number of somethings (beings) united by a common tie
- any portion or expression of matter; stuff of which anything is composed; whatever occupies space and is perceptible to the senses in some way; mutually (with the speed of life) interchangeable with energy, $E=mc^2$
- that which disappears as movement and appears as silent stillness in death. "O for the touch of a vanished hand." (Alfred Lord Tennyson)
- the visible whitecap in the ocean of existence (Hans Peter Dürr)
- living experience of being body...site of being alive. Where will you be, body, in the year 2050?
- shape, sound, color, odor, texture, rhythm, particular, changing
- incarnation, essential matter
- the organ of all my perceptions

From different observers, different generations, different experiences, come different speakings of body:

Jodie, who is now 21, started acupuncture treatments with me when he was six years old, before he quite understood that we die. Recently he was pondering out loud about being alive. "What is this body?" he said. "Why do you put those needles there? When I have a headache and you put a needle in my foot, what are you doing with my body? With this body I play tennis and run and work out. I go to the dentist in it, and I remember my mouth and teeth. Without body I couldn't be here. And with it, everything I do is here, right here, right now. I am the way life lives. I am this body living, and I call it me — smelling, seeing, tasting, touching, hearing. How could I ever not be here?"

Margaret, who is 89, said, "Dianne, you are the only one who touches me now, and in your touch I remember that I am still here, still in a body. You will see as you get old that what you have called 'body' changes unceasingly, that a kind, human touch is simply one body reminding another body that we are here at all, that in body touching body we recollect some unity of being that's always here, that's been here all along."

In *The Woman Beneath the Skin,* Barbara Duden describes discoveries she made in the records of an 18th-century German doctor, Johann Storch. Doctor Storch kept thorough records of his conversations with patients, and in these personal stories of hundreds of different women, Duden discovered a very different "body" than the body learned by any of us brought up in the 20th-century Western world. In mid-life, for example, a time when contemporary women are concerned about their changing menses, Storch's patients gave no special attention to their monthly periods; they dwelled on different concerns, indicating a different experience of body than women born two centuries later.

Duden came to see our modern body as a construct, not a certitude. There is no *is* body—body as a "physiologically stable entity" or an unchanging biological reality.

There is, however, what we say and believe about our bodies. And whatever we assume and say about ourselves as body becomes the ground for our perceptions in living. Let's consider, for example, the word "menopause," a bodied experience in a woman's life, each woman unique.

Our contemporary American culture has largely defined menopause as an illness to be medicated, a pathology to be diagnosed. Therefore, rather than perceive the changes in our bodies as simply nature dancing us, women learn to perceive those changes as a sickness. Duden speaks of this perception as the "invention" of menopause. In our culture we hear menopause described as a failure to have menses, a diminishment of vitality, an attack of heat surges, a sleep disturbance, an irritability and anxiousness, a forgetfulness and poor concentration, a tiredness.... These are all conclusions about a phenomenon. A phenomenon, not a problem: menopause.

Who will be the observer-practitioner to remind me that, depending on what I say, a "hot flash" can be a dazzling phenomenon of being in a body, a "teacher" of life as torrid, thrilling, and fierce—not puny, and necessarily comfortable? Who will remind me that I get a say in how I describe "tiredness"? What if I design "tiredness" as a wisdom guide to call me to stillness, rest, and peacefulness; to call me to simply being, rather than so much doing; to call me to the practice of listening deeply to the mystery of existence? What if, instead of assuming "sleep disturbances," I stop fighting for sleep and design nightly practices of silence and contented (friendly) wakefulness?

This poem from Lucille Clifton offers us another view on (menopause). (Let's place parentheses around the word to remind us of our role as the definers and redefiners of a phenomenon.)

to my last period

well girl, goodbye,
after thirty-eight years.
thirty-eight years and you
never arrived
splendid in your red dress
without trouble for me
somewhere, somehow.

now it is done,
and i feel just like
the grandmothers who,
after the hussy has gone,
sit holding her photograph
and sighing, *wasn't she*
beautiful? wasn't she beautiful? [2]

In 1970 in Singapore with Bob Duggan, during the Hindu festival of petition called Thaipusam, I witnessed more than 500 people put steel skewers through their faces and arms and legs. Each had prepared for this event weeks ahead with fasting and ablutions. Each was in a trance. Each walked in procession, praying to a Hindu deity. And as they finished the ritual, their families and friends helped them pull the steel rods from their bodies. There was no blood, no wounds, and ostensibly no pain. In observing that astonishing phenomenon, I became a new observer of body. No longer a certitude, body became an inexhaustible mystery of matter, of existence. This was before I began to study acupuncture with its little steel rods!

I intend this writing to reveal that our living is in a body, and that what we say about our body determines our experience of living. With me, dear reader, you are pondering and redefining "body." We are calling each other to be observer of body as phenomenon before making any conclusion or telling a story about it. We are "yoohooing" one another to wake up to that we are here in our "horse," our "house," our "hound"—body, our "good bright dog."

On the Circle, Choices

The world is a rotating wheel.
It is like a Dreidel, where everything goes in cycles,
revolving and alternating.
All things interchange, one from another and one to another.
Rabbi Nachman

For this entry in our dictionary, dear reader, our word is "circle," a word to awaken the observer in each of us as we embody the daily round, the round of the seasons, and the round of our lifetime. On our round together, I will speak something. So will you. Until we come to our final word.

Now we are living—and *speaking* the living. Anything we say is a circling and a shining on the Great Circle, from and to the Great Oneness. Anything we do is an offering on the altar of our common union. We have birth and death in common. We have daily life in common, too. Just as *every* wave is ocean, *every* life is Life itself. And every word each of us speaks on the daily round shapes the life we all share.

Rather than say to others "How old are you?" practice asking "How many cycles of seasons have you been around?" This is a reminder for us beings of the human sort that we are one with nature; that we are always on the circle somewhere (regardless of whether we like it or not); that nothing occurs which is not part of the circle. We needn't get off the circle, fix something, then get back on the circle. Everything already is an ingredient in ONE, and thus we can declare peace with being alive, exactly as we are, exactly as life shows itself to be.*

Martha, 91 cycles of seasons, has claimed that peace. At our last acupuncture treatment, resting on the treatment table with eyes closed, she said in a whisper of breath, "Ahhh. I could go now. I am at peace with my whole life. The circle is complete."

CIRCLE:
- cycle
- round, move around, daily round, come round again
- revolve, rotate
- pivot
- wheel
- vortex
- movement
- great dance
- embrace
- return, Eternal Return
- homecoming
- whole
- the Great Oneness

The circle penetrates all life. We see it in the wondrous cycles of nature…in the tide coming in and going out…in the seasons returning, returning, returning. It appears in the mysterious, circling movement of breath…in out, in out…the baby in her sleep, so still…is she breathing?…movement almost imperceptible, in out, in out. My sister Peg's husband, Bob, dead in bed next to her as she awakens one morning in Creation…no longer in the recognizable movement of living-breathing, having breathed out and not in again…one being's cycle complete, returned to stillness.

Life is movement. This is the practiced, living, breathing definition of life from the bones of the ancient Chinese (i.e., human) philosophy. Life is on the move! The Chinese character for life portrays the lid of a rice pot moving up and down, up and down, activated by the steam of the cooking rice. This is *ch'i,* the movement of being, life that shows itself moment by moment and which we observe through our senses, life that moves in the great circle of the seasons and the smaller circles of daily existence.

*I have used words in this paragraph that we've defined in our other dictionary entries (Observer, Body, Phenomenon, Word, and One). By wording the world wakefully —a task we take seriously and joyfully —we are building the world together.

[64]

...a love knot, a cross stitch
of living matter...
Nothing stays put. The world is a wheel.
All that we know, that we're
made of, is motion.[1]
Amy Clampitt

In the village in the village in the village
life repeats itself, life repeats itself.
There is sunlight; there is darkness. The dark
repeats itself, the light repeats itself;
planting repeats itself, harvest repeats
itself. Yet life is never dull. It pats
the drum-hide of the night and is satisfied.
It listens for footfalls when the dogs bark
in the village in the village in the village...[2]
Andrew Oerke

The sun also rises, and the sun goes down,
and hastens to the place where it arose...
All the rivers run into the sea, yet the sea is not full;
unto the place from whence the rivers come, thither
they return again...
Ecclesiastes

As we practice perceiving life as movement, as we practice recognizing the ongoing never-ending cycling mystery of our existence, as we practice observing our own ups and down (like the rice-pot lid) and our ins and outs (like breathing) and what we say about it — we can then practice peace with all our steps, raggedy and smooth, in this dance that we're all in together, this dance of one great rhythmic circling pulse.

John, 33 cycles of seasons, has been coming for acupuncture since he was 18. In a lament he said to me, "Dianne, all I do is get up in the morning and go to bed at night, and in-between I eat, I go to the bathroom — I put it in, I poop it out. I go to work, I come home from work, I kiss Joan my wife, I pet Josie our dog, I feed Josie and take her for a walk — she puts it in and poops it out! And on and on we go like that, day in and day out."

Smiling in recognition of this human song, I also take seriously the wail (howl) of this unique-in-all-the-world being of the human sort, this John within my gaze, knowing that he has come to me for good counsel, that whatever I say to him will matter to him and all the life his life touches. Knowing too that we must all bear life as it is, I reply, "And, what do you say, John, about this daily dance, this dance that one day through death will be otherwise? What do you declare about it now? Heaven or hell? *You* get a choice in what you say and how you dance, moment by moment. I say, choose heaven."

A pause, then John speaks. "Got it. Heaven!"

With all those before us and all who come after us, we join in the circle of life; we dance the sacred dance. Alive and awake for some moments in time and space, we make our offerings one to another before returning to the silence, to the stillness of all movement as we have come to know it...

And the circle of life continues.

> In harmony with the Tao...
> all creatures flourish together,
> content with the way they are,
> endlessly repeating themselves,
> endlessly renewed.[3]
> *Lao Tzu*

NOTES

1. From "Nothing Stays Put" by Amy Clampitt, in *The Collected Poems of Amy Clampitt* (New York: Alfred A. Knopf, 1997).

2. From "In the Village" by Andrew H. Oerke, in *Symphony Number One & Seclected Poems* (Lewiston, New York: Edwin Mellen Press, 1999).

3. Lao Tzu, *Tao Te Ching*, translated by Stephen Mitchell (New York: Harper & Row, 1988), excerpt from #39.

In the Oneness,
We Are All "Friend"

Camerado, I give you my hand!
I give you my love more precious than money,
I give you myself before preaching or law;
Will you give me yourself? Will you come travel with me?
Shall we stick by each other as long as we live?[1]
Walt Whitman

You, reader, I call you "friend," whoever you are, wherever you come from, whatever you look like, however long you've been living. As you are reading this, you are breathing. So am I. As you are breathing, you are living. Me too. As you are living, you are simply dwelling here on earth until the moment you breathe out and not in again. The same for me. We are beings of the human sort, alive at the same time. And, though I do not know you, that is, though I may not have smelled, seen, tasted, touched, heard you—the unique you of this Oneness—I bear with you what it is to be alive, the conditions of being and the concerns about being.

We are not abstractions. We are each a specific, unique, embodied and ancestored presence. Having been born into the world of existence, we each have learned our own ways of being. And yet, maybe there is no stranger, no foreigner among us—only different ways of being, different views, different speakings. Not opposite ways, just distinct. Each distinction an epiphany, a "shining" on the whole.

So then, what are we creating here, alive and awake together? That's what this essay is about—having "our say" about life as friendship.

FRIEND:
- "Another I." (Zeno)
- "A friend is, as it were, a second self." (Cicero)
- "A single soul dwelling in two bodies." (Aristotle)
- Companion, one with whom we break bread—*com-pane*.
- Partner in bearing living and dying.
- Reciprocity as the practice for one's life. "What you do not want done to yourself, do not do to others." (Confucius)
- "Love one another." (St. John)
- *Philia,* that is, goodness, love. "In the presence of *philia* we come to know ourselves as more beautiful, true and good." (Plato)

Friendship is a way of being. It is a practice. Of his practice of friendship the Dalai Lama says, "I try to treat whomever I meet as an old friend....It comes with daily practice...[it is the practice of] love and compassion, interconnectedness, regardless of circumstances....The need for love lies at the very foundation of human existence. It results from the profound interdependence we all share with one another."[2]

Jesus's story of the Good Samaritan is a story of friendship: A man is on his way down from Jerusalem to Jericho and falls into the hands of brigands. The robbers take all he has, beat him and then make off, leaving him half dead. A priest comes down the road, followed by a Levite. Both see the suffering man, yet do nothing to help him. At last a Samaritan traveler comes upon him and is moved with compassion. He bandages the man's wounds, pouring oil and wine on them. He lifts him onto his own mount, carries him to the inn and looks after him. The next day he takes out two coins and hands them to the innkeeper. "Look after him" he says. "On my way back I will make good any extra expense you have." (Luke 10:29-37)

Caring, that is, thoughtful action, lives at the heart of friendship. The Samaritan uses his presence, his actions and his treasure to care for a fellow human being. This is a story of gift, not business deal, not strategy. Not sentimentality, not indifference. Caring is action, one unique being with another in the circumstances of living—a call to human kindness that awakens goodness and summons camaraderie.

We are born helpless, all of us. Without gracious friends, we could not have made it this far, none of us.

In most of our modern homes, we are not dwelling within the sound of church bells, nor cowbells, nor each other's dinner bells. For many of us, these sounds no longer exist. So what calls you awake, "Camerado"? What summons us to friendship, to life as holy, as connected, as nature? What calls us to each other? The buzzes, rings and signals of our high technology do not arrive at rhythmic and ritual times like monastery bells calling for daily lauds, noontime Angelus and evening vespers. The cellular phone call arrives any time and place, and yet its ring is always a signal that one being of the human sort is reaching out, calling out to another, not unlike the bells of old.

These days, who will be the observer reminding us that every ring, every buzz, every reaching out could, if we say so, be a wake-up call to friendship, to living together, to seeing each other through?

I have a friend, Lynn, who intentionally sets her wristwatch to beep at noon every day, no matter where she is, as a wake-up to peace and oneness in the "village." If she is with others, as an act of friendship she invites her fellow "villagers" to a moment of peaceful silence. This is Lynn's practice, her "bell," her "yoohoo" in being. She designed it.

Yesterday I received a "courtesy call" that I knew would end up in a solicitation for money. Just as I was about to go into my usual barking frenzy, I woke up to the phenomenon that there was a human being on both ends of the phone! I hear, "Hi, Dianne, I'm Mike. I'm a fireman here in Howard County, and I'm calling to say 'thank you' for your support last year." I said, "Mike, do you mean it?" and "What do you enjoy about your work?" He addressed me by name, and I did the same with him.

Mike said that he loved being with his team of fire-fighter friends and, with them, helping others out of danger. He told me that he has learned to respect the power and beauty of fire, the ways of fire and water and earth; that he doesn't really "fight" fire as much as "dance" with it so it doesn't go out of control.

So I said, "Mike, treasure for treasure. I'll add a bit more to my last year's gift and thank you for your friendship in this call. I am now more awake to life as gift."

"Dianne, my Grandma Coleman taught me to be a friend to everyone. She said we're all in this together. And she really lived it, with no embarrassment." Then Mike laughed and added, "Who taught you, Dianne? Someone did. You are the only person today who did not cut me off. I am grateful."

Recently, as I was traveling to get home on a snowy day, I signaled to change lanes. There was a lot of skittish traffic around me, folks with concerns about the road and the snow. A young woman driving next to me motioned for me to get in front of her. She slowed down to let me in. She smiled. In that moment, that simple act of friendship on this road we share together became, to this observer, all that being alive together is about.

So, in the spirit of the Dalai Lama, in this the We-llennium, our first gift of friendship is the declaration of Oneness with each other, this "other I."

I close this essay for now, "Camerado," with an offertory of loving friendship:

I thank you, my friend. I breathe. I breathe with you. I bow to you simply for being.

I give you my listening, friend, with no judgment, simply listening to the phenomenon you are in the deep mystery of existence.

I see you, alive and awake, and I will see you right through to death, my friend.

I celebrate you. I am your friend and you are mine, enjoying the passage of time and the lightness of being together.

I savor the sweetness of you, dear friend, and the songs of life that sing you. Let us share the bread of human concern these days of our life.

SO BE IT.

NOTES
1. From "Song of the Open Road" in *Leaves of Grass,* by Walt Whitman. Modern Library Edition (New York: Random House, 1993).

2. *Tibetan Portrait: The Power of Compassion* (Rizzoli International, 1996). Phil Borges (photographer) and the Dalai Lama (text).

In the Oneness: Summer, Winter, Living, Dying...

I have always known that at last I would take this road
But yesterday I did not know
It would be today.
Peter Matthiessen

In the circle of seasons, summer is across from winter—the heart of blooming and the heart of frost, the dance of flowers and the stillness of snow, the laughter of friendship and the hush of listening to the mystery of existence—two distinct facets of the same jewel of being alive.

Growing up, I used to think that I was more mortal in the winter, when the freezing Northern New York air surrounded me, and that I was less mortal in the warmth and play of summer. It is not so. We are every moment mortal. And no one of us is more mortal than another. Ever. We all go to death. That phenomenon balances our differences.

Our word, beloveds, for this entry in our dictionary is "death." We are deeply involved in this word. Life is the mystery of being embodied. At the end of life, our only body will let itself loose. How do we grapple with a world in which the word "death" lives—a world where we who ask about death are profoundly, inextricably bound in the question?

Death. Death. Death. My Mama Irene is dead. She stopped. She ceased. She is extinct. She is no longer in her body. Death came for my mother. I saw it. She breathed out and out and out and out and not in again, on the 12th day of March, the year 2000, at 5:00 A.M., that once-only, will-not-happen-again day in creation. Mama went out of breath. That breath never again, yet that moment lives forever. She expired. Now she has disappeared, out of sight, sound, taste, touch, smell. I will never see her again embodied. How could this unimaginable finality be so? What do I say here? What is sayable in the Great Stillness, the Great Silence, the no-more-movement, no-more-sound? How do I dictionary this word for you, my breathing beloveds?

We are a breath that passes. (Psalm 61) Breath marks our time here on earth, from the very first inspiration until we breathe out and not in again. Lifetime is breath-time. Breath defines time. Time is breath. Every year we pass a silent anniversary of a day we cannot yet know, the day of our last breath. We beings of the human sort breathe, then we name it "time" as each breath comes and goes and comes and goes and comes and goes. My mama has no more breath, no time left.

The word "death" reveals the word "being." These words live together in the world. In the face of death we can *do* nothing. We must learn to *be.* We must practice being. Just before his death, my friend John said, "When I'm *being,* simply being, I am in love. Being and loving are the same thing." Then he put into words something I had not yet heard. John said, "Being, loving and dying are the same, Dianne. They are all one. Practice *being.* I am in love and ready for death every moment, with any breath. Don't forget this, Dianne. Tell everyone."

John defined death as his practice of being. Life and death come together. Our only say is not "do we die?" Rather, our say is what peace, what oneness, what practices we bring to our death *now,* while we are here, living. In Japan there is a practice of writing a death poem, a kind of love song to life. As people recognize their closeness to death, they write some words to convey their being in that moment.

As you realize your call is coming, what will be the last words from your lips? We can establish them at any moment. What an awesome practice to bring to daily life *now* the words we would want to die with—our last speaking before the great silence of death, a gift to honor the elders and serve the children. Words like "appreciation," "oneness," "beauty," "compassion," "partnership," "loving-kindness," "acknowledgment," "peace," "listening," "hallelujah."

In certain Buddhist traditions, the practice of remembering death is simply saying each day, "Death is real. It comes without warning. This body will be a corpse." A Native American friend, Mary, upon waking in the morning, practices declaring, "Today is a good day to die."

French phenomenologist Gabriel Marcel wrote, "We cannot hide as stark and massive a thing as death, no matter how much we sanitize, anesthetize, homogenize, mechanize, institutionalize, and medicalize it." Death may go unrevealed throughout the day, even the night. Yet often in the late quiet of darkness comes a sometimes terrifying awareness of its being, inescapable.

Perhaps such moments are our wake-up calls. Perhaps what we label "insomnia" and "sleep disorders" we could rethink as our reminders, our "yoohoos," temple bells awakening us to being. All of our symptoms move us closer to the mystery of death and the mystery of being alive, every "squawk" a reminder we are here. Sometimes our suffering is the only "yoohoo" we have in a day to call us back to being. Every symptom can be designed as a teacher for living and dying.

MAMA'S PROMISE

I have no answer to the blank inequity
of a four-year-old dying of cancer.
I saw her on t.v. and wept
with my mouth full of meatloaf....

Sometimes I lie awake
troubled by this thought:
It's not so simple to give a child birth;
you also have to give it death,...

Then I think of Mama,
her bountiful breasts.
When I was a child, I really swear,
Mama's kisses could heal.
I remember her promise,
and whisper it over my sweet son's sleep:

When you float to the bottom, child,
like a mote down a sunbeam,
you'll see me from a trillion miles away:
my eyes looking up to you,
my arms outstretched for you like night.[1]
Marilyn Nelson Waniek

Mama, I bear your death. I bear the oh-my-god of being alive while you are no longer. I fall to my knees and howl, leashed to you forever. O my beloved, my Mommy Girl, our Mommy Girl—all six of us born from your loins and oh-so-many more born from your abundant, generous love. In this mystery of your life and passing, I will never again forget to be astonished about Being. Thank you, Mama. I love you so. I want to hear again the way you ate a potato chip, and how you made buttermilk sound so good as you drank it. Without you, Mom, in the ways I knew you to be, I am learning to live within you, surrounded by all the beauty of being that you loved. And we, the rest of us still here breathing, still have each other's deaths to bear, and each other's lives to tender.

> …we stood and watched the fire of my mother's life rise
> high above the crematorium, dissolving into blue sky…
> growing light and lighter until no trace remained…
> this body, her body, our body, moving everywhere now,
> touching everything, becoming everything.
> *Stephen Hyde*

> When the time comes to face death…we have to return
> to the silent source of our life and stand up there. We have to come
> back to the realm of oneness and make it alive,
> with a feeling of togetherness with all sentient beings
> and a deep understanding of human suffering…
> *Dainin Katagiri*

When death comes, we have to go. Each of us and all of us. We are truly One in this. Whatever our beliefs, traditions and stories about "passing," the phenomenon is that each of us will breathe out and not in again. None of us knows which will come first—our death or tomorrow. Oh, so astoundingly, so ongoingly astonishing! We are still here breathing, beloveds. Death has not claimed us yet.

And until that day, we practice…*being*.

> Love is anterior to life,
> Posterior to death,
> Initial of creation, and
> The exponent of breath.[2]
> *Emily Dickinson*

NOTES

1. Excerpts from "Mama's Promise" from *Mama's Promises,* a collection of poems by Marilyn Nelson Waniek (Baton Rouge: Louisiana State University Press, 1985).

2. "Love," in *Collected Poems of Emily Dickinson* (New York: Gramercy Books, 1982).

With Each Breath, Time…
to "Practice Eternity"

In the last piece, Beloveds, we talked of "death"—which brings us to "time," our word for this entry in our dictionary. In these entries we make distinctions through which we build the world. These distinctions are not "final." There is no final word on any word as long as languaging beings still breathe. Rather, we look at what a word has meant to others, what it could mean, and what we make it mean now for our conversations, our "turnings" together. The words in our dictionary thus far: Conversation, Observer, Phenomenon, Conclusion, Declaration, Practice, Beginner, Word, One, Body, Circle, Friend, Death.

So, Beloved Reader, what shall we say about the word TIME? Are we inventors of, keepers of, spenders of, prisoners of this word? If we say so, we are. What phenomenon does the word TIME point to? What world resides in the word? Where do we locate TIME?

> Behind Me—dips Eternity—
> Before Me—Immortality—
> Myself the Term between—
> *Emily Dickinson*

We beings of the human sort breathe. As each breath comes and goes, comes and goes, comes and goes, we name it "time." Breath marks our living here on earth, from the very first inspiration till we breathe out and not in again. We could call life "breath-time," for breath outlines and defines our being here. Every year we pass a silent anniversary of a day we cannot know yet, the day of our last breath, the end of our time. This day couples another day that we *do* know, the day of our first breath—our birthday—the beginning of our time.

We are a breath that passes.
Psalm 61

We *are* time. We are *living* time. We make it up. What do we define with each new breath for the sake of each other, for the children and the ancestors? With each word, each breath, each moment, we are choosing what matters in time.

Time presences opportunities for tending each other, for giving each other our listening, our being. Every class I teach, I begin by ringing the bell. I stand still and silent in front of each person and sound the bell for each. As I go around the circle, I am sister timekeeper, yoohooing each student to being, to being *here,* to the opportunities of embodied time, this *now.*

...a lifetime burning in every moment...
...and all is always now...
T. S. Eliot

In the treatment room, Anna told me she was going to have a face-lift. "I don't want to go back very far, just a few years," she said, "so I can look 45, not 55." "Aging" is a word that lives in our human conclusions (mostly hidden) about time. We buy what the ads call "age-defying products." We are in a fight with wrinkling, changing, being. Can we—I, too, at 64 cycles of seasons—experience this face, this body, this being, simply as phenomenon, exactly as I am? Can we give our aging selves the same freedom to be—and the same awe—we grant to a newborn baby?

If you realize all things change,
There is nothing you will try to hold on to...
Lao Tzu

Everything changes. Everything. My face, your face, the dog, the trees, the ground, the roses... What abides? The young boy becomes the old man, the young girl becomes the old woman. *And yet we are every moment home:* some strand of being abides in every moment. *Now* is any breath. *Here* is anywhere... "now, here, now, always... (T. S. Eliot). *Forever* lives in this once-only-will-not-happen-again moment.

As a way of revealing our own hidden conclusions about time, let us continue to speak of time in terms of breath, and through this practice presence awe, Oneness, eternity. Here is an example close to me: In the months before my mama died, all the way through her suffering to her last breath, through all the changes, when anyone asked how she was, my youngest brother Andy would always say, "She is so beautiful. She is so beautiful." Exactly as she was, simply being, she was beautiful. Exactly as *we* are, just being, breathing here, we are so beautiful...timelessly.

I have no fight with Anna having a face-lift. I will remind her, no matter what, of how beautiful she is, no matter how many breaths she has left, no matter how she perceives her appearance. If she lives 110 cycles of seasons (which may become the lifetime norm) at an average of 900 breaths per hour, Anna will have 433,620,000 breaths between now and when she breathes out and not in again. Breath-time—it is what we all have right this moment, our share, our unique quickening.

The question is not how many breaths do we have. The question is what gift will we make of our life—our breath? For listening? For thanking! For creating, for joying, for singing. Mama Irene, with her 664,176,000 breaths, made of her life a love song for peace. I know. I lived in her breath.

"Time" is a word, our invention, a distinction we use day in and day out ("day" itself is an example of how we divide our living into segments). As a construct, time can hardly be revealed: it is like water to fish. Like fish we swim in notions of intervals, of seconds, minutes, hours, days, weeks, months and years, of chronology and measurements, of age and wrinkles, of beginnings and endings. We begin our stories with "once upon a time," and say things like "I don't have enough time," "time is running out," and "for everything a time." "Someday I'll have it all together," we say, or "I'm getting old." We speak of nighttime, morningtime, sometime, anytime, everytime. We talk about time as though it means something, yet there is no IS time, IS like a fact. There is only our living, bodied experience of being—and what we say about it. As observers, perceivers of existence, conscious of being, we have created time. Time is of our making.

> Time gets foreshortened late at night.
> Jesus died a few days ago, my father
> and sister just before lunch. At dawn

I fished, then hoed corn. Married at midmorning,
wept for a second. We were poor momentarily
for a decade. Within a few minutes I made
a round-trip to Paris. I drank and ate during a parade
in my room. One blink, Red Mountain's still there.[1]
Jim Harrison

Red Mountain, the Grand Canyon, the squirrel hanging upside down to get at the bird food—these have no use for time. Time doesn't mean anything apart from what we make it mean. It is a distinction constructed (like a red stop sign) to call our attention to being here—together, alive and awake.

We are, in each moment, making the choice that matters. Will we choose to "practice eternity," to presence Oneness, to give our gifts to others? My Mama Irene chose to spend many moments creating joy in her kitchen. She was practicing eternity.[2]

Each distinction that we single out from the Oneness, like time, is a guardian of the Oneness. Each marking is a little wake-up to being here at all. Each wording we make points again—though sometimes obscurely—to our existence together as one. *E Pluribus Unum* we have written on every piece of our money: in many, One. One in many.

With words we build a vocabulary of existence, distinctions, markings, for living together. A red stop sign does not grow on a tree or under a rock. It is a human marking left on the landscape that we are not alone, that we are here with each other, and that our individual actions matter to the whole.

In each moment of our life, eternity. Eternity in all the moments of our breath. With each breath, a choice…

NOTES

1. Jim Harrison, "After Ikkyu #19" from *The Shape of the Journey: New and Collected Poems*. Copyright © 1998 by Jim Harrison. Reprinted with the permission of Copper Canyon Press, www.coppercanyonpress.org.

2. The phrase "practicing eternity" is from Lao Tzu, and appears in passage 52 in Stephen Mitchell's New English Version of the *Tao Te Ching* (New York: Harper & Row, 1988).

Human, Being in Love

Love…
It is a word:
speaking it, we speak
ourselves…
Octavio Paz

alive we're alive
we're wonderful one times one
ee cummings

Each one's himself,
yet each one's everyone
Theodore Roethke

Several years ago, I led a workshop in New York City for about 45 people, none of whom knew each other. About 10 minutes into the opening conversation, a woman stood up, looked around at the other participants, and spoke to them in a strong New York accent. "My name is Nina, and I'm a tough New Yorker," she said. "I don't talk like this—like we're talking here—and I don't think like this. But I'm in love with youse guys!" Others nodded their assent, and someone said out loud, "It's kinda like we're getting married and moving in with each other. I don't even know your names or any 'scoop' about you—and I'm marrying you!"

Later that same evening, I was eating dinner by myself in a restaurant when my waiter, José, from Costa Rica, asked if I would like to see a photo of his beloved. "Of course," I said. He showed me a picture of a beautiful girl and told me she was his daughter. José said that when he realized she had been conceived, he had changed his whole life so he could be with her and take care of her, whatever that required.

I am pondering MARRY as a word for our dictionary-for-living. I remember José's love for his child and Nina's connection with folks she had just met and "married"—and I choose the word Marry, a vocabulary word for being together. It joins words we have defined in earlier essays, words such as One, Body, Friend, Death, Time—words through which we are redefining being alive together on this earth.

Wherever a word is, there a human being is, or has been. Wendell Berry, in the title of his book *What Are People For?* asks what we "beings of the human sort" are here for on the earth. What do we bring to being? What are we meant to bear on behalf of the whole, the Great Oneness? William Blake offers, "We are put on earth a little space that we may learn to bear the beams of love." What could that possibly mean for us in our daily round?

Let's design something for "bearing the beams of love" as we explore our word Marry. Note that by Marry I do not mean two of us having a wedding. I mean all of us together, beings of the human sort, in Love.

We are born babies, children of humans, bearing a humanity that can suffer and cry and laugh and even die. We arrive bodied and helpless, in need of one another. We could not have made it to this moment without each other. Our ongoing arrival, our coming to life this day occurs in our mutual presence. We are breathers in concert, simultaneous, side-by-side, *tutti insiemi appassionatamente,* all of us together in human kindness, opening room for the existence of each other, accepting that we are in the human company, companions in living. What can I do alone?

We are kin in the simple work of being; kin in the supreme mysteries of coexistence: I–Thou (Martin Buber), little you–I (ee cummings). We are thinking, heart-beating, breathing beings of the human sort, each unique, all one. And we are dwelling together on the earth, our home. "Building Dwelling Thinking," says Heidegger. We are learning to "marry."

Instead of living separate isolated lives, we can, as a declared possibility, live together thoughtfully as ONE. In some human tribes, even dreaming is done on behalf of the collective. From the very beginning, from our birth into these bodies, we have come into friendship, that is, into the beauty of being here together; of "seeing" each other through—right through to death; of learning to be one with the whole world and every being that has ever lived.

In other words, we are learning to Marry—to wake up and know that we are here together, and to claim our kinship. In this use of the word, Marry means any loving action of living together here in the world, choosing and practicing ways of being, of loving. It could be said that love is the declaration of our union.

Life and Love are not over yet…we are still here. We still have a say. For the sake of each other and the arriving children of us humans, what Life are we? What Love? Do we love, shall we love, each other? Will you Marry me now? Shall we cultivate Life, cultivate being alive together as ongoing Marrying with each other—our children, our friends, our parents—as Native Americans teach us to say, the Great Oneness, Wah Do, "all our relations." Aren't we all in this together, really, together in the mystery of existence?

> Let love be at the end…
> *Lucille Clifton*

As a practice of making room for you as partner, Dear Reader, whoever you are, whatever your circumstances, however life is living you, I address you as Beloved—and I do so sight unseen, smell unsmelled, sound unheard, taste unsavored, flesh untouched.

I assert that we today are practiced in a vocabulary of opposition: "fight cancer," "kill the legislative bill," "do battle with disease." We attack with our words: this versus that, me versus you, us versus them. We fight our symptoms, our aging, our death, our differences. We live in a language of reaction and conclusion, the vocabulary of antagonist and adversary. Such a discourse does not allow for the possibility of oneness and friendship.

Marry reminds us to walk in this world giving our gifts to each other— offerings of acknowledgment and gratitude, of listening and reassurance, of new "seeings," of joyful partnering, of thoughtful caring—gifts that point to and remind us of our oneness—gifts that call us to make a language for revealing oneness.

In the realm of high energy physics, we are already married, already One. Lecturing on quantum physics, Hans Peter Dürr, Professor of Physics at the Max Planck Institute in Munich, speaks of life's oneness as an ocean, and of us as temporary whitecaps appearing on the ocean for a hundred years, more or less. Though we look and act and sound and smell so different from one another, we don't have to go very far down in the whitecaps before realizing that we are ocean, already one, that we are simply showing as separate. We belong to each other already, and we are still here to be one with each other, to Marry, that is, to *wake up* to our union.

The way we bear whatever is asked of us this day matters to all of us. Being alive is profoundly personal, yet not private. We are temporary whitecaps on the ocean of existence, requiring compassion and loving-kindness. We know we will disappear back into the ocean one day, and none of us knows when. Now is our time to love each other.

> Earth's the right place for love:
> I don't know where it's likely to go better.
> *Robert Frost*

Here is an example of Marrying. I offer it in the form of a teaching story from Ivan, blinded at 11 by a ball that hit him on the head. He is now 58 years old, married with kids, and his kids have kids, so he is a grandfather. He does acupuncture for his living.

I gave a workshop that Ivan attended. In his presence, I realized how awake I was to having eyes to see with; so I turned to him and said, "Ivan, this blindness is profoundly personal— *and* it is not private. You are suffering it on behalf of all of us. How I know this is that I have never been so aware of having the gift of sight as in your presence. Thank you, Ivan, for bearing this on our behalf."

Around the room, participants nodded and murmured in agreement. Ivan, visibly moved, responded, "Thank you for saying that. I was feeling so isolated, thinking I was the only blind one and that I didn't belong here." Then I asked him to speak to us about how it is to bear this blindness—and bear it on our behalf (this was a whole new thought to him).

With hardly a moment of hesitation, Ivan stood up, "looked" around the circle slowly and deliberately, and spoke. "You don't know what you are missing— the beauty and wonder of the sounds and tastes and textures and smells of life. Of course I want my eyesight back," he said. "And *you* do not know what you are missing."

Ivan spoke about the courage of his mom and dad as they bore with their son's circumstance. He spoke about the ease and lightness of being that his children and his children's children have with him. None of them, he said, take the gifts of the senses for granted.

Truly, in just a few minutes, Ivan had presenced the essence of the workshop: that we are in oneness; that we are here together, not alone; that everything we bear is for the sake of each other; that how we bear what life brings us matters to the whole; and that the ancestors and the young ones — all of the generations — go together.

In coming full circle with Ivan, I asked if he would allow me to bow to him. He hesitated. I told him the bow was meant to honor his parents, his children — my gratitude to all of what and who he is. For the sake of the generations, he said "yes." Realizing that he could not see me bow to him, I asked if he would allow me a not-so-usual way of bowing, that is, to get down on my knees and kiss his feet. Would that be all right? He graciously said yes, and I kissed his feet—a thank-you for bearing "our" blindness with such grace.

Gift given. Gift received. A Marrying.

As we walk in the world in the declaration of oneness, we are compelled to think different thoughts and take different actions than if we walk in opposition. In choosing the word Marry, I am bidding us to create practices through which life shows as One—with plenty of celebration of diversity, that is, oneness showing in myriad ways.

First and always we begin in the One, which is a classic definition of Marry. And so, to our conversation we add the verb Marry as an action word for bringing forth the world together. We have, all of us, more Marrying to do.

Anamnesis—
Recollection of Being,
Remembrance of Things Past

All our heart's courage is the echoing response to
the first call of Being, which gathers our thinking
into the play of the world.
Martin Heidegger

…there is nothing lowly in the universe:
I found a beggar:
he had stumps for legs: nobody was paying
him any attention: everybody went on by:
I nestled in and found his life:
there, love shook his body like a devastation:
I said
though I have looked everywhere
I can find nothing lowly
in the universe…

I…stood in wonder:
moss, beggar, weed, tick, pine, self, magnificent
with being![1]
A. R. Ammons

The word we explore in this essay, dear reader, I first heard through the voice of historian-philosopher Ivan Illich. It is not used in common speech. Yet, I have designed it as a "yoohoo" that wakes me up to the phenomenon of being alive. When I am most forgetful that life is a gift, most hohum about having daily breath and bread, most squawky and complaining about existence, most thinking that something is wrong and needs to be fixed—this is the word that I use to bring myself back to the oneness and awe of life, exactly as it is. This word is Anamnesis, often translated as "recollection." It is derived from the Greek—"calling to mind again," "remembering."

Cherished reader, when did you first recognize that you are here? What experiences yoohoo you into being? To elucidate Anamnesis, I'll share with you two of my recollections. Both occurred when I was nine years old. The first was when I went into the room where my father lay dying. He had brain surgery for a tumor, and though his eyes were open, he showed no recognition of me. "Daddy, can you hear me, can you see me, do you feel me touching you?" He looked like my father, yet he didn't act like my father. Where is my father? In that moment I woke up to being in this body. I was overcome by this mystery of living.

The second vignette took place a month after my dad's death. I walked into the fourth grade classroom of St. Joseph's orphanage, not knowing anyone. Sister Mary Marcella, the teacher, called me to her and took my hands into her own. She then ever so slowly and gently kissed each of my hands and said, "Welcome, Dianne Mary Connelly." Up until then I do not remember ever hearing the sound of the whole name that means me. I am here. I am welcome here, hand-to-hand, worthy of being, worthy of being—kissed. So are you. I am in awe. Right now. I remember.

I hold the human privilege of wording the world as a sacred honor, and so it is not okay to say just any old thing about being. I take seriously Heidegger's statement that our forgetfulness of being is in our speaking. I think of Barbara Duden's book, *Woman Beneath the Skin,* in which she reports how women in an eighteenth-century community spoke of their bodies, and I ponder her vigilance in pointing out how we have learned to live diagnostically. Culturally, we have learned to look at being alive as a pathology, forgetting simply to be together without labels, without diagnoses, without judgments of dysfunction, malformation, or bad design. It is so easy to speak in language of what is wrong, not language of simple, mutual presence.

From the very moment of waking up in the morning and recognizing that here I am, one more round, I am determined not to miss this experience of existence, determined that it be the direct, here-I-am-now experience—not an interpretation of being, but a smelling, hearing, seeing, tasting, touching of being. I intend that being not be hearsay.

I use this word Anamnesis to recall me to existence without labels, existence as a recollection of being, a remembering of consciousness.

One of the great stories of the world is about Buddha, that is, the one who woke up to being. In recognizing that we are bodied beings who can get sick, who age, and die, Buddha considers deeply how shall we be, and what shall we say about being while we are here, and how do we help each other along the "being way." It is usually in a moment of crisis that we become conscious of the possibility of not being, and therefore conscious of being. And in such a moment we are usually more open to what ancient wisdom, such as that in the Buddha story, can teach us about how we "be."

When a person comes to me for treatment, what is she coming for? What is she asking from me… Is it to diagnose her, to give my view of what she thinks is wrong with her, that is, to "sentence" her according to me—to characterize, identify, and describe her? Most of us have imprisoned ourselves, sentenced ourselves to death already in our characterizations and self-descriptions.

Laura, age 47, came to see me for "asthma," a diagnosis given to her years ago in the presence of her concerns about breathing. "I have asthma," she told me. "I am asthmatic." She had constructed the idea that she "had a problem," and now wanted acupuncture to help her fix it, since other treatments such as Prednisone had so many unwanted side effects. As she spoke, I could hear Laura's forgetfulness of being. The words she used to tell me about her pain and concerns were creating her as an individual isolated, alone, and afraid, separate from the oneness of being.

Like all of us, Laura entered this life as an infant with no constructs, no distinctions of separateness. Yet living in the company of other beings of the human sort, she learned from them their interpretations of what it is to be. And, along the way, she had forgotten (or not learned) the possibility of other interpretations. She got lost, as in the opening line of Dante's *Divine Comedy: Inferno:* "Midway through the journey of life, I found myself alone in a dark wood astray from the straight path…" Like Dante and Laura, all of us are tellers of the stories of being.

Laura had not come for me to diagnose her; she had come for Anamnesis—

for me to remind her of being. So, to move us to a new starting point, I told her the old adage, "My barn having burned to the ground, I can now see the moon." I asked her if she could see any "moon" in all that she has had to bear. Laura was quiet for a time. Then she said, "Well, I *am* grateful to have breath at all, and to be able to breathe. I do not take it for granted. And then there's my friend John—he's been with me several times during an asthma attack. The other day he thanked me for always being the reminder to him that we are here at all. He took my face in his hands and said, 'I am so happy to be alive at the same time you are.' I guess that's a kind of 'moon' from my asthma," she said. "I just never thought of it like that. Is that what you mean, Dianne? I guess I've been pretty busy concentrating on the burning barn. I forget there might be any bigger picture."

Yes, Laura, and there's no fault in forgetting. It simply means we must design practices for remembering. So I asked Laura whether she might use this experience, our conversation about the moon, as her "yoohoo" to remember to be awake during *this* day in creation, this once-only, will-not-happen-twice day of our breath.

From there, Laura and I talked more about how and when she has been wakeful to being. When did she first "know" that she is here, and that one day it will be otherwise? What was her first recollection of being? And who are the persons with her in life who benefit from her being alive and awake? Who receives an offering from her suffering?

Pain is always a matter of being. As we spoke, Laura kept realizing that her squawks, her symptoms, her upsets, have also been moments of awakeness to being, moments when the mystery of existence was unavoidable.

Such recollection of being, illustrated here by Laura, is what I have come to call a practice of ANAMNESIS. Essentially, it is simply being, *remembering* being, and speaking it—and therefore, of necessity, speaking poetically. That is, using words wakefully as pointers to the "moon," to oneness, to the awe of existence. ANAMNESIS is a practice of bringing present in the moment the awareness of breath, of heartbeat, of constructs and past thinkings about being here—all of them as callings to more and more consciousness. From this point of awareness we can, in the words of the SOPHIA mission statement, "come to life more fully, so as to serve life more wisely and more nobly... sagely stillness within, sovereign service without." Being is deeply personal, *and* it is not private. We all belong to Being.

"Not *how* life is—that's the mystical—but *that* it is," wrote Wittgenstein. The practice of ANAMNESIS is about not forgetting the wonder of being, ever.

It is about recovering from our amnesia. It is about awe, about consciousness. From this point forward, we can and must design daily practices for staying conscious, new ways to end our forgetting. A small example: if you wear a watch, switch it to the other wrist, now. In its unaccustomed place, you have designed the watch as a wake-up call to being.

We are exploring the word Anamnesis in the springtime, the season that shows itself to be a giant wake-up call. In spring, we awaken newly to life as creation—new seeings, new possibilities. We can ask new questions through which we become more skilled observers of being: Could we be in awe without being in complaint? Could we distinguish the phenomenon of being from our conclusions and interpretations about being? Could we grant being to each other—mutual presence, reciprocal company, remembering our living at the same time? Could I have life with you, and death? Shall we dance? Could we? Would we? When?

Yes. Yes. Now.

NOTES
1. Excerpt from A. R. Ammons's poem, "Still," is from *The Selected Poems: 1951-1977,* expanded edition, W. W. Norton & Co., Inc. Copyright 1986 by A. R. Ammons.

Gaze — A Gift that Grants Being, Allows Goodness and Beauty to Show

...with an eye made quiet by the power
Of harmony, and the deep power of joy,
We see into the life of things.
William Wordsworth

...now the ears of my ears awake and
now the eyes of my eyes are opened
e.e. cummings

My eye is in love.
Frederick Franck

You think you see, but you don't.
The day you really see, you will weep.
J. R. Worsley

I SEE the sleeping babe, nestling the breast of its mother;
The sleeping mother and babe—hush'd,
I study them long and long.
Walt Whitman

In a childhood accident with a paring knife, my mama lost her right eye. During my growing up, she wore a glass eye, and she almost always wore sunglasses, indoors and outdoors, whether the sun was shining or not. As a kid, I was never quite sure how and where to look into her eyes, forgetting which eye she could see with.

From time to time, a glass eye company sent samples to Mama. I was fascinated with those inert "eyes" in the box, and would look at them secretly. I remember shuddering and wondering if they could see me, or even see something mysterious beyond me. I thought they might even be gazing at eternity, and, as a little girl, eternity was a very big thought. It remains so, a word of mystery and continual contemplation. My mama's glass eye taught me what a gift it is to see, what a gift it is to be alive and awake.

Dear Readers, I am choosing the word Gaze around which to build our conversation, to construct together not certitudes, but a little "thinkery." At this very moment, where are your eyes? What are you doing with them? Who are you being with them? What is it you call "seeing"? And in this moment, what is it you call reading? Could we use the word Gaze to mean having our eyes present to each other as gift, seeing the being of each other through all our myriad differences? These are some questions for us to stir.

Gaze yields the certainty that we are alive at the same time. If we are gazing, we are here. By Gaze I do not mean a hard, staring, peering, greedy, grasping, indifferent, or voyeuristic use of my eyes. I mean using my eyes to behold you—to hold you in being—not to assess, explain, or diagnose you. To gaze is to shine on you and grant you being. By Gaze I mean the practice of looking wakefully and lovingly with my eyes. It is the opposite of prejudice.

To Gaze is to practice seeing the face of the beloved everywhere, in everyone, seeing your face as beloved, exactly as it is. Gazing allows us to see beauty, grace, oneness. It is an action of our whole body's attention, a long, pure look, being truly present—looking "long and long," as Walt Whitman writes it. It is saying I see you, I include you in my gratitude for being, in my accepting the mystery of being, in my seeing new possibilities for being, in my joy and celebration of being, in my thinking into the sweetness of being.

Without each other's Gaze, we have no place to bring forth the world, no place to share our stories of being, no place to practice waking up, no place to practice Anamnesis—to practice our recovering from forgetting, our returning from our amnesia. Gazing is a practice of anamnesis. Eyes cannot see themselves. We need each other's eyes to see ourselves, to recall who we are.

When my 10-year-old patient Mikey comes for an acupuncture treatment, he says, "Let's play that eye game." When we first met, I taught him to look into my eyes, and from that he made up his own game. We both close our eyes, and he says, "Now, open." We look at each other as softly as we can until he says, "Now, close." We repeat this three times. Then Mikey says again, "Now, open," and this time we both look out the window. Without talking, simply being still, we look out at the trees together.

Mikey lives in the world having been labeled "hyperactive." He, like the rest of us, needs to be called to remember that we are here with each other, and here for the sake of each other. Mikey can and does gather me up in his eyes, and I, him; we give each other the looks of oneness, of compassion, of kinship; the looks of love. It is a practice to cultivate our gaze. It is a practice to make sure there is no "ho-hum" about being alive together. In cultivating the use of our eyes, Mikey and I are practicing being together.

Meister Eckhard says the eye with which I see God is the same eye with which God sees me. Gaze *is* attention, and attention *is* prayer, say the great mystics who practice finding things to love. Gazing is an act of finding company, not living in isolated aloneness. I think of words in a song sung by Ysaye Barnwell of Sweet Honey in the Rock: "…there were no mirrors in my Nana's house…and the beauty she saw in everything was in her eyes…"

Always there is something or someone in front of our open eyes. Teilhard de Chardin told this story: "One day—I was still under ten—I stubbed my toe against a pebble. I picked it up and I loved it." Loving a pebble… We are "linked to something by the very fact that it *exists*. Nothing is beneath notice, everything reveals the All, everything aspires to the All. Love is the felt, inner face of the affinity mutually binding and attracting the elements of the world. Love is that universal convergence by which the universe falls passionately in love with itself."[1]

Tamar Amani Star is here on earth. He is 11 weeks old now, my grandboy. I gaze at him. The miracle of his being blazes, resplendent. In his presence it is easy to open, to belong to love, to look in wonder. I gaze at the presence of god in the breath of this baby, in his very flesh. Blessed be you, holy matter. With open eyes. He is simply being, with eyes open, to everything, to everyone.

Caeli, my 13-year-old daughter, says, "Mommy, will you write about Forte?" (Forte is our 100-pound, three-year-old Chinook.) "What shall I say, Honey? Shall I tell how he points his snout straight up into the air and sniffs the great outdoors like a prince breathing in his kingdom? Shall I speak of his gaze as he sits in the grass, one paw over the other, wagging his tail and looking with open eyes?"

Forte is being a dog and Tamar is being a baby. Dog and baby are not doing. They simply be. All their movement comes from being, with no assessment, preference, opinion, unbeing, no thought of right or wrong, no attempt to figure anything out. I take them as my teachers as I learn to gaze.

Pa, my farmer stepdad, has taught me, too. One day we stood gazing out at the cows in the pasture, and he said to me, "Look at those cows, Dianne. Never a bad arrangement."

I must learn to gaze. I declare gazing as a practice of being. I say it is a practice of being in the world so that goodness and beauty show—a practice of using our eyes for one another.

NOTES
1. Pierre Emmanuel quotes Teilhard de Chardin in the foreword to the *French Catalogue*, compiled for the 1983 Centenary Exhibition on Teilhard's life and work.

Language—Speaking Being, Making the World

...all our lives calling out, "This is my name!
This is my name! Can you hear me?
Do you hear my voice? Who are you? Speak!"
Agnes De Mille

HAIKU
love between us is
speech and breath, loving you is
a long river running
Sonia Sanchez

A word spoken creates a dog, a rabbit, a man. It fixes their nature before our eyes; henceforth their shapes are, in a sense, our own creation. They are no longer part of the unnamed shifting architecture of the universe. They have been transfixed as if by sorcery, frozen into a concept, a word. Powerful though the spell of human language has proven itself to be, it has laid boundaries upon the cosmos.[1]
Loren Eiseley

A trio of baseball umpires is sitting in a bar. The first says proudly, "I calls 'em like I sees 'em." The second takes a swig of beer and says, "I calls 'em like they is." The third sets his beer

down and slowly says, "They ain't nothin' 'til I calls 'em."
Source Unknown

As I ponder our word for this issue, Language, I am intending to be evocative, to ask us to think together, if not new thoughts, at least some not oft-spoken thoughts that call us into more wakefulness about being, about being here alive at all. This article is a little three-page toe in the ocean, a tiny contribution meant to "yoohoo" us into being.

The phenomenon of language can be invisible as air, little thought of, unrevealed. That was so for our family until my brother Jack stopped being able to speak coherently. It was during the afternoon of our Mama Irene's last breath that her firstborn, John Anthony Connelly, lost language. He still had breath and sound on breath, yet he could make no meaning for a listener, nor could he write his own name. Now, a year later, he can say the days of the week and most of the months. He was a college professor. Language was his life.

Yet, one of the most beautiful uses of language was in my brother Jack's words on that very day that language left him and thus amplified the usually hidden phenomenon that language is. During the last breaths of our mother, Jack motioned for me to stand with him, and we put our hands to our heads in the form of salute. Then he spoke: "A great and glorious human being is passing." Those were his last clear words.

> How is it the tiger has stripes? It is the deep nature of tiger. How
> is it the human being speaks and listens and speaks and listens? It
> is the deep nature of human being.
> *Chinese Adage*

We are given breath. We make language linking human to human. We give voice with our breath—making sounds of the human tribes, the many human tribes. In our language we make love, war, indifference, compassion. Paul Celan, the great poet, took his own life after the Holocaust, unable to bear the language that gives rise to both the horrifying and the holy. Language holds the power of breath. Language is a complex phenomenon by which we shape creation, articulate being embodied, and observe being. Everything we say is something about being. We are immersed in words, which create the text of our lives, the context for our existence. Words are the makers of our world. Each language is a distinct world, not merely the same world with different labels.

We, as speakers and writers, listeners and readers, are the heartbeat of language. Every word, phrase, sentence, and discourse presumes the presence of beings of the human sort at some place, some time. We are profoundly involved in the worlds we are wording. Our bodies are affected by language all the time. We are moved to actions by each other's speaking. The world of advertising depends on it. The world of lovers depends on it. The world of parents and children depends on it—instruction, agreement, description, praise, quote, question, request, bear witness, organize.

Tamar, my grandboy, is now four months old. He does not say "house," "tree," "dog." In fact, he doesn't "say" anything. He sounds, he babbles. And he is changing his sounds week by week and sometimes day by day, always changing. Born into the possibility of language, he does not yet talk, nor can anyone give him talk. Like walk, he must take it on himself. He must body it. No one can do it for him. Living in a household with him I observe cries, coos, gurgles, squeals, squeaks. Tamar has not yet formed a word, though his sound-on-breath quickly gets interpreted into story by those of us around him, especially his cries: he is teething, he is tired, he needs to be changed, he's hungry, he's in pain…

Everything we say and everything we write is something about the phenomenon of being here at all, tongues sounding in 6,000 languages, all saying something about being here, shining on existence, interpreting, making meanings for our human concerns, sensations, needs, thoughts.

One of these concerns is language itself. Many languages are becoming extinct. That is, as new generations are no longer learning these languages, they will be lost. Not unlike my brother Jack's loss of language.

> Speech is a river of breath, bent into hisses and hums by the soft flesh of the mouth and throat.
>
> *Stephen Pinker*

A young woman, 24 years old, recently started acupuncture treatment with me. She has not spoken since her mother and father died in a plane crash three years ago. Before that time, Jeannie spoke fluently in English and in French. On hearing her story, I thought about Buckminster Fuller, who after the death of his daughter went to the edge of Lake Michigan to do away with himself. Though he did not commit suicide, he later said, "I did die that day." For two years he was silent, not speaking as he fashioned himself newly into being alive. And I thought about language, especially about what is clear in the vivid ballet of sign language—that each of us is embodied, a languaging being, living with all the conditions and circumstances of being bodied including sickness, aging, and death.

We could say that Jeannie is undergoing an experience with language. She is bearing what she must bear, enduring something that touches her innermost being and her outermost existence, in the presence of which she is speechless. No word or combination of words matches what life is asking of her. She must marry death, as we all must. O what is sayable? In the face of this mystery, what is our voice? Are we not all mute, stilled?

Here is where we each become poet at the edge of being, languaging the impenetrable, unfathomable, inexplicable presence of life, using words to point to what cannot be said. Poetry calls us back to the silence from which all words come. Our everyday speaking hides the wonder that we are here and the wonder that one day it will be otherwise. We know not when.

> Our forgetfulness of being is in our speaking.
> *Heidegger*

Holding her silence dear, I asked Jeannie if she would ponder one word to live in for the rest of her life, a word that would honor her mother and father, a word of her choosing. I told her that the Sufi say the first word is "ah," and all the rest blossom forth from that. I read her the Stanley Kunitz poem, "Passing Through," written at age 82... he is now 95.

> ...gradually I'm changing to a word.
> Whatever you choose to claim
> of me is always yours;
> nothing is truly mine
> except my name. I only
> borrowed this dust.[2]
> *Stanley Kunitz*

We are languaging beings, bodied, mouth to ear, ear to mouth, my mouth, your ear, your mouth, my ear. Sharing with you is inherent in language...this is my voice saying your name, this is your ear listening. In *The Tree of Knowledge*, Maturana and Varela write, "everything said is said by someone." They remind us that each of us, as a languager, is a particular, unique someone in a particular place, saying something about being, speaking a version of the Tao according to each of us. For no speaking is abstract, disembodied. It is always from some body in some particular time and space. With our words, we bring forth a world. We are the languaging ones, the beings who write poetry and sing. Let us say then — because we still can say — something that is worthy of this breath, this our shared gift of being.

This is Dianne speaking. And I assert we have only this world that we are creating with each other, a world constituted and continually becoming in language. Change the language and we change the world, the view, the perception, our ways of being. This language, dear reader, includes the words mercy, loving-kindness, compassion, thank you, ah.

Ah…

NOTES
1. Reprinted with the permission of Scribner, a Division of Simon & Schuster, Inc., from *The Invisible Pyramid* by Loren Eiseley. Copyright © 1972 by Loren Eiseley.

2. Excerpt from "Passing Through," in *Passing Through. The Later Poems, New and Selected* by Stanley Kunitz (New York: W.W. Norton, 1995), page 131.

Smile is a Medicine Word

...i have lived forever in a smile...
e.e. cummings

Life doesn't cease to be funny when people die,
any more than it ceases to be serious when people laugh.
George Bernard Shaw

It could happen any time, tornado,
earthquake, Armageddon. It could happen.
Or sunshine, love, salvation.

It could you know. That's why we wake
and look out — no guarantees
in this life.

But some bonuses, like morning,
like right now, like noon,
like evening.[1]
William Stafford

I began writing this entry in early September, having chosen to define the word "smile" for the dictionary we are building together. Then life asked us to bear September 11, 2001. Life asked us to stand deep in the question of being of the human sort, all 6.5 billion of us, with no pretense, minimizing, or excusing.

Yet I choose to keep the word "smile" for our dictionary this time—especially now. For even in such excruciating, unbearable pain, even in sacred seriousness, even now, we are not cut off from joy, from that which is practiced with a smile.

Smile is a word for living. It belongs in our medicine pouch as a daily practice, as a gift, as a way of life. I have been practicing smile upon meeting another along the daily way—in the street, driving up at a stoplight and looking over, in the elevator, at the breakfast table.

Smile is defined as an expression of joy by the countenance, from the Latin *mirari*, to wonder. What shall I put on my countenance for you, on this face I cannot even see, yet belongs already to your eyes? A smile is never abstract, never disembodied. It is observable, observable like the sun shining. It is good medicine. Better than a drug, more contagious than a virus, Smile is a crucial gift for each other, a kindness in the presence of our human cruelties, a compassion amidst our human atrocities.

Smile is a word for us living together. It is a word for seeing each other through, whatever life asks of us this day. We are in this world to love it, to smile with tender affection on the commonplace things of this life, to body forth a deep and radiant inner joy, no matter what.

In this writing, I enter with you into mystery—the gift that is the mystery of being alive together, the gift of friendship as we companion one another in our speaking and listening to each other. Accompany me in this teaching story from my beloved Mama Irene:

A few days before she died, we, Mama's six kids, realized that not one of us had mentioned death to Mama, not wanting her (or us) to be frightened by talking about it. So, the following day, I sat with her as she moved in and out of sleep. "Mama," I whispered, "are you talking to God?" "Yes," she said, clear as a bell. "Is He calling to you to come to Him?" "Yes." So clear she was. "Are you ready to go?" "I think so," she said. "Mama, last night we all talked, and though we will miss you so, we want you to go to Him when your Love calls." There was silence for what seemed like a very long moment. Then she said, "That's good. And, don't forget, none of you are that far behind me!" I not only smiled, I laughed out loud. One more time Mama had shined on life and illuminated it for us.

I am done with great things and big plans, great institutions and big success. I am for those tiny, invisible, loving, human forces that work from individual to individual, creeping through the crannies of

the world like so many rootlets, or like the capillary oozing of water which, if given time, will rend the hardest monuments of pride.
William James

This *is* the question of being alive—for what do I give my daily breath? This is a serious inquiry to face, since none of us is getting out of here alive. We are giving our life today, so what do we say matters, today?

I wonder as I observe a brokenness in our humanity, our interdependence— how is it so that we beings of the human sort are doing terrible things to one another? We are all suffering, bearing our circumstances, globally. We are all, from whatever tribe, defining what it is to be alive. We are all asserting something about being here together, and the assertions are not the same.

More than ever in our lifetime, reader, we, the tribes of our earth, are calling to each other. For what would you kill another? For what would you say, "everything else I can bear, but not that"? For what, for whom, would you give your life? For what, whom, do you give your life now, and how? These are our questions, beloved reader. They are not rhetorical, and they are not trivial.

> ...I say unto you...joy and sorrow are inseparable....
> When you are sorrowful look again in your heart,
> and you shall see that in truth you are weeping for
> that which has been your delight...
> Verily you are suspended like scales between
> your sorrow and your joy.[2]
> *Kahlil Gibran*

The autumn leaves, so beautiful, falling to the earth, as they must...calling us, the participant observers, to awe, to breathtaking, breath-giving wonder, calling us to the precious beauty of existence, to the sweetnesses, shinings, smiles, sorrows, sobs for all creation. I overheard the conversation of a young woman whose husband was killed on September 11: "If I sleep or laugh or enjoy something, I feel I am letting him down." She was struggling to put her sorrow about him together with her joy, to bear that she is still here breathing while he is not, to celebrate the gift of their happiness in the time they had alive together.

No one is exempt in the journey from birth to death, and we cannot delegate it. We must present ourselves. There is no safe seat in the audience. Life is living all of us, each of us, and none of us knows what this day will bring for us to bear. We have the joy of each other's company until we don't, and then we have the recollected joy and presencing of what we loved together.

On the phone with Pa, my farmer stepdad, I ask, "Pa, are you smiling?" "Yes, daughter, are you?" "Yes, Pa. Are you missing her, Pa?" "Like breath itself, daughter. I'd walk a million miles for one of her smiles."

> If I die, survive me with such sheer force
> that you waken the furies of the pallid and the cold...
> I don't want your laughter or your steps to waver,
> I don't want my heritage of joy to die.
> Don't call up my person. I am absent.
> Live in my absence as if in a house.
> Absence is a house so vast
> that inside you will pass through its walls
> and hang pictures on the air.
> Absence is a house so transparent
> that I, lifeless, will see you, living,
> and if you suffer, my love, I will die again.[3]
> *Pablo Neruda*

Grief is a call, not to anger and war and upset, but to awe and gratitude and joy. Let a smile stop you in your tracks. Let it be an unexpected help in an intricacy of living. Let it be as easy to smile as to frown. See it as a simple gift ongoing. Smile in the midst of uncertainty, of unknowing, of upset, of concerns. In their wedding vows, my son Blaize and his beloved Lisa spoke these words as their ongoing practice with one another: "I promise to bring you laughter and joy, and to smile every time that I see your face."

Forte, our dog, easily wags his tail. Tamar, my grandboy, easily coos and smiles. These little moments of beauty live with our tears of anguish. All of us are worthy of grief and joy. All of us. We cannot medicate our sorrow, nor can we dispense with our lightness of being. We must rejoice and be glad that we are here at all with each other, in the heart of the matter of existence. More awake. More conscious of companioning one another to create new discourses for living in oneness in our global village, bearing with one another, turning our sufferings into offerings.

Maybe our most radical help in the bearing of life is the practice of joy. So smile. Now.

Because you can.

NOTES

1. William Stafford, "Yes" from *The Way It Is: New and Selected Poems.* Copyright © 1991, 1998 by the Estate of William Stafford. Reprinted with the permission of Graywolf Press, Saint Paul, Minnesota, www.graywolfpress.org.

2. Kahlil Gibran, *The Prophet* (New York: Alfred A. Knopf, 1989).

3. Pablo Neruda, "Sonnet XCIV," in *Pablo Neruda: Absence and Presence* by Luis Poirot, translations by Alastair Reid (New York: W.W. Norton, 1990).

Sing Our Way Home

Who makes me sing when my voice is silent?
Songs have left me for places unheard.
Who bids me sing when all singing seems useless?
Woman hold my hand, woman hold my hand...
Bernice Johnson Reagon
SWEET HONEY IN THE ROCK

From the throat of the woman who keeps on singing,
day rises nobly evaporating toward the stars...
all the silent voices in her voice...
the sorrows of this world...
Gabriela Mistral

Sing yourself to where the singing comes from.
Seamus Heaney

One of my earliest recollections is of being nine years old in St. Joseph's Orphanage after my father died. Every morning the nuns (Grey Nuns of the Sacred Heart) sang prayers for the day in Gregorian chant, their arms outstretched. As a kid, kneeling in the chapel, I heard this daily cadence of Latin sounds. What I can say now is that these were moments of beauty, of wonder, of awe... moments when sorrows and joys were one, tears and smiles united ...moments of peace in a little girl's world.

Through the years, chanting and singing of all sorts have been a continual presence in my life, from Native American chants to the sounds of Tuvan throat singers and Tibetan monks, from the African *Missa Luba* to the Gregorian Magnificat and Ave Maria. Recently, I found through my friend Allegra in England a motet by Thomas Tallis, *Spem in Alium*, which weaves together voices singing 40 parts all at once, each distinct, yet forming one magnificent whole. I hear the singing as a majestic call to all of us who dwell on earth—a call to the many to dwell as one.

SING is our word for this entry in the dictionary we are creating together. In choosing an entry, I look at the words I use daily in conversations, words that evoke discourses based on the ancient wisdom at the root of our School of Philosophy and Healing in Action (SOPHIA). Sing is such a word. It is a medicine word. It, too, like our last entry Smile, belongs in our medicine pouch. To SING is to connect, to belong, to remember beauty, to be inspired. Singing (and listening to singing) are two practices of being alive and awake.

In Australia, the Aboriginals "sing" the world into existence. Bruce Chatwin, in his book *The Songlines,* writes:

> Aboriginal Creation myths tell of the legendary totemic beings who had wandered over the continent in the Dreamtime, singing out the name of everything that crossed their path—birds, animals, plants, rocks, waterholes—and so singing the world into existence....
>
> ...each totemic ancestor, while travelling through the country, was thought to have scattered a trail of words and musical notes along the line of his footprints, and now these Dreaming-tracks lay over the land as "ways" of communication between the most far-flung tribes....
>
> By singing the world into existence,...the Ancestors had been poets in the original sense of *poesis,* meaning "creation." No Aboriginal could conceive that the created world was in any way imperfect.[1]

There are so many ways of singing our life into creation. In the treatment room my patient Carolyn—a woman of middle age, recently widowed, her children all grown—despaired of her worth. She had forgotten that she has a say in designing the next steps of being alive and awake with life's new circumstances. I sang to her. I held her head in my hands; and to the tune of *O Tannenbaum* I sang, "O Carolyn, O Carolyn, how lovely life is through you." I thought it crucial that in this moment she remember herself as a song of life, as a melodious and wondrous possibility, exactly as she is.

James is a little boy, six years old, and he loves to sing "How Much is that Doggy in the Window." He learned it from his grandma, who sings it to him every time she sees him. I know James through our time in the treatment room. His folks wondered if acupuncture might help him learn to stay dry through the night. You could say he is practiced in wetting the bed. He is not as practiced in staying dry. As I thought about James loving to sing "Doggy in the Window," I had an idea. With his enthusiastic cooperation, we constructed a "treatment" together. The song, we agreed, would be his "peepee" song, and it would help him to peepee in the potty. Though it may sound silly to adult ears, he changed the words to "how much is that doggy in the peepee." He laughs and laughs when he sings it on the potty. Where the practice of "staying dry" may have had some struggle with it, his gift of song brings some lightness and peace to the process.

We could say that James is a baby buddha awakening to being, and awakening to his own power to construct ways of being as he lives day by day. I did not use a needle with this little boy. I simply did a treatment using three moxa on "Stone Gate" (a point on the lower abdomen) as a reminder of his strength (the stone), and as a reminder of his ease (in the way a gate moves easily to and fro).[2] The point itself is a song, a poem of being, which he has had his whole life. Touching the point at this time in his life "matches" the song of what he is learning at six years old. I see that this is a good way to speak about acupuncture points—as songs, as poems of being which, when touched by a needle, by moxa, by hand, are reminders of who we are as the breathing between heaven and earth, as the singing that brings peace and calls us home.

For two hours each month, Dr. Ysaye Barnwell, a member of the a cappella ensemble of African American women called Sweet Honey in the Rock, holds "Community Sing!" at the Levine School of Music in Washington, D.C. Lots of folks from all over the area gather there for an evening of singing. One could say we are "strangers," though the Dalai Lama would say we are simply "friends who haven't met yet." Within minutes, Ysaye guides us into five- and six-part harmony. It is as though we had sung together all our lives, a glorious experience of being human. In song we experience "human" as one, as good, and as beautiful. These two hours of singing are wind in my sails for the month. I use them to goose me to remember goodness and beauty… and to keep singing…every day.

O Ma Rainey,
Sing yo' song;
Now you's back
Whah you belong,
Git way inside us,
Keep us strong…
Sterling A. Brown

Whatever workshop I am teaching, wherever I am—a funeral, a birth, a wedding, a gathering of any sort—we sing together songs of oneness, songs of partnership, songs of life's movements. Often, we sing "Row, Row, Row Your Boat." We sang it at John's memorial, a song so appropriate for a man who dedicated himself to assuring that everyone has clean, clear water. We sang it at Mike and Carrie's wedding, the round reminding us to row gently as we flow together down life's stream. And at Dede's memorial service, we celebrated her gifts of joy with the perfect line: "merrily, merrily, merrily, merrily." Almost everyone in our American culture knows this song. Some elder taught it to us. And we, likewise, pass it down the generations, singing our way.

Dear reader, practice the gift of song. Let your mother and your father hear you sing. Let your children hear you sing. Let your friends hear you sing. Listen to them sing. Sing to them. Sing with them. Sing them into existence.

Let us together sing our way home.

The strongest and sweetest songs
yet remain to be sung…
Walt Whitman

NOTES

1. Bruce Chatwin, *The Songlines* (New York: Viking Penguin, 1987), pages 2, 13, 14.

2. Moxa is a plant, *Artemesia vulgaris,* sometimes used in treatment. A small cone of the powdered herb is placed on an acupuncture point, lit and allowed to burn down until the patient begins to feel the heat, then removed quickly so as not to harm the skin.

Alive and Awake —
This Day, Every Day

Every day is a god, each day is a god,
and holiness holds forth in time. I worship each god,
I praise each day splintered down, splintered down
and wrapped in time like a husk,
a husk of many colors spreading, at dawn
fast over the mountains split.
I wake in a god. I wake in arms holding my quilt,
holding me as best they can inside my quilt...
Today's god rises...[1]

Annie Dillard

Our word for this essay is an invisible word, maybe even a forgotten word, yet one that encircles our being. My intention is to reveal the word, and the awe of being that is held by this particular little three-letter piece of our English language. Like any word, it is simply a finger pointing to the moon, a saying of something about being that points to Being itself.

Annie Dillard calls it "God's tooth." We are born into it. We live and have our being in it. Everything we do is held within it. Mon, Tues, Wednes, Thurs, Fri, Satur, Sun, good, to, some, every, yester, birth — all are prefixes for it. There is nothing to do with it except to live it, and then, when the call comes, to die in it. We were born into its light and dark, the 24 hours of a round, our quotidian. This word is Day.

Day marks the earth's rhythmic roll. It is a word that binds us to time, that gives us a container in which to dance the mystery of existence. It is our time of breath, our opportunity for living, our opening for love. It is *this* day, this once-only, will-not-happen-twice day in creation, this revelation that we are here, awake to being alive and awake.

Before doing, going, having, we are here awakening, recurring in these bodies this day. This is the first phenomenon of existence, that is, we exist now. You are reading this, so you are not dead yet—you have this day. I am writing this, so I am still here. I have this day—dawn and dusk, mystery of light and dark, sunrise and sunset. Today we are alive again to sing and laugh and cry the sorrows and joys of existing at all, as light breaks and dark falls, as dark breaks and light rises.

My grandmother Clarenda's old milk jug comes to mind when I ponder the word "day." Every day she would wash the jug before the milkman came to fill it up again. Hers was not an era of throwaway containers. The simple vessel itself was held to be useful, purposeful, and beautiful in the realm of daily events. I remember that for the children it was an honor to dry the jug with Grandma's special dishcloth. "All in a day's time" she would say about whatever she was doing on her daily round. And often, about something important to her, she would say, "We must sleep on this."

Grandma saw the whole of living as One—all of it, the ups and downs, the fillings-up and the emptyings-out, the wakings and sleepings. Everything was contained in a day: her daily bread and breath and breadth, her morning and her night, her joy and sorrow, her being and doing. Her day was a jug for everything that has to do with being alive—all in a day's time.

We are here, now, recurring in these bodies filled with breath. Day is for our living. Each moment, everywhere, Day is present.

Every class I teach, I begin by ringing a bell as a call to being fully present on this day in creation; and I say, "this once-only, will-not-happen-twice day." One morning, Rose, a student at Tai Sophia Institute, was late for class. When she arrived, she was in tears—and in awe. Rose said that on her way to school, an oncoming vehicle had crossed the median into her lane and "totaled" her car. During the moments of the accident, she said, "I was so awake to *being* here. Now I really know why Dianne starts every class the way she does. Today is not a ho-hum. I am alive and awake this day. It could be otherwise."

This day we are having a unique and unrepeatable experience of the world.

And, I assert, we are making constant comment about this day without revealing the gift of it—comments about whether I like the weather, how I think those wrinkles on my face look, how long it takes for the traffic light to turn green, what you think of me—as though just any old commentary matters in our book of hours. I can and must design how I speak of this day and how I use this day; and I must design it without yet knowing what will be asked of me.

How are you designing this, your day of days? Let us help each other design practices that reveal and define this day as the container for living together in oneness. Here are some of my offerings:

This day is for awe. I am in practice to be grateful, in wonder.

This day is for stillness. I am in practice to listen to the mystery of existence.

This day is for goodness. I am in practice to use my eyes for seeing beauty, to see newly.

This day is for joy. I am in practice to smile with warmth and lightness of being.

This day is for thoughtfulness. I am in practice to savor and sing the sweetness of creation.

And, what I do with this day, belongs to you.

And, what you do with this day, belongs to me.

And, no one of us knows now what life will ask of us.

We do know we will have to dance until we run out of days.

> From birth which brings us into the light of day,
>   like the bud on the branch of a peach tree,
> to the night of our burial which returns us naked
>   to the original void,
> there is nothing but change and transformation.[2]
> *Neijing Suwen*

NOTES

1. Annie Dillard, *Holy the Firm* (New York: Harper & Row, 1997). Copyright © 1977 by Annie Dillard. Reprinted by permission of HarperCollins Publishers, Inc.

2. Claude Larre, *The Way of Heaven (Neijing suwen, chapters 1 and 2),* translated by Peter Firebrace (London: Monkey Press, 1994).

With Each Breath,
Awaken to Life

Human being is a breath that passes.
Psalms 104:29

We are breathing together. While doing anything we are breathing—outbreaths, inbreaths, like waves of the ocean, our perpetual movement of being, almost imperceptible. Our lifetime is based on breath; it is our treasure, our bottom line, our condition for being alive, for everything we do. Upon this breath we build all of living.

Our word for this little toe-in-the-ocean entry in our dictionary for living is BREATH. Like a finger pointing to the moon, this word points to the most ordinary, extraordinary action of our daily life. With each breath we are in the world, creating the world. With each breath we put the past away and open to the next astonishment. With each breath we are *alive*. By revealing this simplicity, I assert we are more, not less awake to being.

Ask lovers who experience breathtaking love what "breath" is for. And we are these lovers, each breath a gift of life to itself, each breath a gift of love, simple, unadorned, precious. A kiss is an exchange of breath, a conspiring, an inspiring with another, a breathing together. We marry daily our breath in the mystery of existence. My friend told me the love story of his great aunt and uncle, together so many years. She died in her beloved's arms saying, "Kiss me, just keep kissing me, don't stop kissing me." He breathed with her until he was alone with breath.

> ...I love thee with the breath,
> Smiles, tears, of all my life!
> *Elizabeth Barrett Browning*

Our first breath is a definitive moment of existence. We go from breathing with the blood corded to our mother to breathing the air common to all being. Until the last breathing, the ongoing breathing in and out cradles us, outlines and underscores the wonder of being alive. I think about times when my babies were small and their breath so quiet that I would put a mirror to their nostrils to check if they were still breathing. King Lear speaks of Cordelia in the same way:

> ...Lend me a looking-glass;
> If that her breath will mist or stain the stone,
> Why, then she lives.

And later, realizing she is dead, Lear says,

> Why should a dog, a horse, a rat, have life,
> And thou no breath at all? Thou'lt come no more,
> Never, never, never, never, never!
> *William Shakespeare*

Think of a breath and a deep bow as the same. Sometimes simply the awareness of breath as a blessing is sufficient to call me to the simple experience of being alive and awake in this moment. What if I see to it that every breath is a reminder of the awe of life, an "Ahhh"? Each inspiration is a call to the breathtaking beauty of being. As I give each breath that meaning, it then has that meaning.

John is 46 years old, a pediatric surgeon who comes to me for acupuncture treatment. The label "asthma" brought him to me. When I asked "What does 'asthma' mean to you?" John said, "It means I am very aware of my breathing. I do not, I cannot take it for granted. I have medicine I take to help me breathe." "What is your embodied experience of this 'asthma'?" I asked. He then described sensations of heat and pressure in his upper chest and head, accompanied by thoughts such as "Uh-oh. I'm going to die if I can't get my breath." "I wonder if I can do the next surgery successfully?" "This young life under my hands is depending on me. What if I can't help?"

I asked him if he ever allows himself to be thanked by the parents of the children he operates on. "Usually not," he said. "Usually I'm thinking something self-deprecating, something like 'I took too long—I should have done it in four hours rather than six.'" As John revealed his sentencing of himself, I offered, "Suppose you take 'breathing' and 'thanking' as the same word? What if you simply went still and allowed yourself to be thanked? What if you allowed the parents to bow to you for the gifts you give to their children? They are thanking you for the continued breath of their beloved babies. What if, in a quiet, reflective way, you simply say, 'You are welcome.' In doing so you can call them to remember we are here together, breathing together. You call them to cherish this gift, all the while knowing that someday it will be otherwise and our breath-time will be over." Then I said, "John, you already call all of us to this anyway—life has asked you to be wide awake about breathing in bearing this word-world called 'asthma.' Through you, this wakefulness to breath, to life, belongs to all of us."

Data indicate that one in 20 of us in this country bears some "squawk" about breathing as a chronic concern. "Asthma" and "allergy" have become shorthand words. Even as we use these words as labels for ailments, we must not miss the glory of the phenomenon they point to—our breath. Breath is serious. It weds us to life and death. All of us. Always. All ways.

During the months before she died, my patient Bonnie used her pain as a drillmaster, an instructor. When she felt a wave of sharp constriction in her chest, she practiced coming to attention, absolutely still and alert, expecting nothing, listening to what she described as "babies breathing." She said she felt so free in those moments. She was pure being, doing nothing, simply breathing in the present moment. Bonnie practiced "now" and "breath" as the same word.

I, as you, dear reader, can practice wakefulness with each breath. We could, like Thich Nhat Hanh, the Buddhist monk dedicated to peace on earth, add a word to each inhalation and each exhalation: "Breathing in, I breathe peace; breathing out, I smile," is one example. We can make our own breath prayers to call ourselves to mindful breathing. This day, my practice is to breathe in with the word "love" and to breathe out with "compassion." Thich Nhat Hanh reminds us: "Breathe! You are alive. Keep fully aware of it."

Breath transcends time zones, cultures, and places. It immerses all of us together in air as in a bath of being, a broth of oneness. We could not be without it. It is our quickening. With each breath, the blowing wind of being moves through us.

Student, tell me, what is God?
He is the breath inside the breath.
Kabir